Tailor-Made Marriage

When Your Lives Aren't One Size Fits All

Marita Littauer & Chuck Noon

Tailor-Made Marriage: When Your Lives Aren't One Size Fits All
© 2006 by Marita Littauer and Chuck Noon

Published by Kregel Publications, a division of Kregel, Inc., P.O. Box 2607, Grand Rapids, MI 49501.

All rights reserved. No part of this book may be reproduced, stored in a retrieval system, or transmitted in any form or by any means—electronic, mechanical, photocopy, recording, or otherwise—without written permission of the publisher, except for brief quotations in printed reviews.

Scripture quotations marked AMP are from the *Amplified Bible,* © 1965, 1987 by the Zondervan Corporation. Used by permission. All rights reserved.

Scripture quotations marked MSG are from *THE MESSAGE* by Eugene H. Peterson, © 1993, 1994, 1995, 1996, 2000, 2001, 2002. Used by permission of NavPress Publishing Group. All rights reserved.

Scripture quotations marked NCV are from *The Holy Bible: New Century Version.* Copyright © 1987, 1988, 1991 by Word Publishing.

Scripture quotations marked NET are from the NET Bible®. © 1996–2005 by Biblical Studies Press, L.L.C. http://www.bible.org. Scripture quoted by permission. All rights reserved.

Scripture quotations marked NIV are from the *Holy Bible, New International Version*®. Copyright © 1973, 1978, 1984 by International Bible Society. Used by permission of Zondervan Publishing House.

Scripture quotations marked NKJV are from the *New King James Version.* Copyright © 1979, 1980, 1982 by Thomas Nelson, Inc., Publishers.

Scripture quotations marked NLT are from the *Holy Bible, New Living Translation,* © 1996. Used by permission of Tyndale House Publishers, Inc., Wheaton, Illinois 60189. All rights reserved.

Scripture quotations marked TLB are from *The Living Bible,* © 1971 by Tyndale House Publishers, Wheaton, Illinois. Used by permission.

Library of Congress Cataloging-in-Publication Data
Littauer, Marita.
 Tailor-made marriage: when your lives aren't one size fits all / by Marita Littauer and Chuck Noon.
  p. cm.
 Includes bibliographical references.
 1. Marriage—United States. 2. Marriage—United States—Religious aspects—Christianity. 3. Remarriage—United States. I. Noon, Chuck. II. Title.
HQ734.L596   2006   248.8'44—dc22   2005036170

ISBN 0-8254-3161-1

Printed in the United States of America
06 07 08 09 10 / 5 4 3 2 1

Tailor-Made Marriage

Contents

Preface...9

Introduction: Marriage: A New Script...................13

Part 1: Personal Issues

1. The Fire's Gone Out.................................27
   Personality Differences, Physical Relationship

2. Weepy Most of the Time..............................43
   Depression

3. Childless by Choice.................................54
   Outside Pressures, a Full and Happy Life

4. Growing Apart......................................66
   Different Levels of Maturity, Respect and Honor

Part 2: Career Issues

5. Lack of Time Together 77
   Communication, Creative Time Together

6. Rocky Roads 92
   Job Loss, Change in Life Direction

7. Sacrificed Her Career 103
   Personal Fulfillment, Career Options

8. Career Chaos 114
   Job Security, Depression

9. Twenty-four/Seven Togetherness 125
   Doing Business Together, Separating Business and Personal Life

Part 3: Financial Issues

10. Merging Finances 141
    Prenuptial Agreements, Creating Connectedness

11. Who Pays? Who Plays? 152
    Control, Shared Activities

12. Secret Spending 160
    Agreement on Expenditures, Establishing Trust, Children from a Previous Marriage

Part 4: Ex-Spouse Issues

13. An Excess of Ex's 173
    External Pressures from the Ex, Potential Ministry to the Ex

14. Deep Resentment on a Delicate Subject 183
    Attitude Adjustment, Guided by Guilt

Part 5: Stepfamily Issues

15. Between a Rock and a Hard Place 197
    Disciplining Children, Commitment

16. Finding Your Place 210
    Insecurity, Stepchildren Relationships

    Epilogue: From the Head to the Heart 222

    Appendix A: Your Personality Profile 230

    Appendix B: Directory of Professional Contributors 235

    Appendix C: The Couple's Communication Exercise 240

    Appendix D: Choosing and Working with a Therapist 243

    Endnotes 245

Preface

As I was wrapping up the writing of my book *You've Got What It Takes,* I was working on a chapter called "Celebrate Your Path." The goal of this chapter was to encourage readers to create a mission statement, not just for their professional life, but for their personal life as well. I looked at my own life. I had such a statement for my professional ventures, but I did not have a personal one. I knew how valuable my professional statement was, so I could see the importance of a personal one—as I was recommending to my readers. I mulled this over for several days, focusing on the need for a personal purpose statement.

At the time, I was attending a women's Bible study on the book of Ephesians. As part of my preparation for the study, I would read the assigned chapter in several different versions of the Bible. One night I read Ephesians 5 in *The Message.* I wasn't specifically looking for a personal mission statement, although it was still in the back of my mind. I was simply doing the homework for the next day's lesson.

But, as I read, this verse jumped out at me and I instantly knew it was to be my personal statement—at least for now: "Observe how Christ loved us. His love is not cautious but extravagant. He didn't love in order to get something from us but to give everything of himself to us. Love like that" (Eph. 5:2 MSG). As I read that, I knew my personal mission was to love my husband, Chuck, with extravagance—not to get, but to give everything of myself. As I cook breakfast or dinner, as I do the dishes, as I do the laundry, I can give something of myself, not expecting to get in return. At that time, Chuck was in a tough place professionally. He was not in a place to be able to give much. But I was. I wrote that verse on a card and placed it on my bathroom mirror to remind me of my mission. Even now, years later, I find that I have to frequently repeat this verse to myself, as doing what it says is contrary to my human nature.

Shortly after embracing this idea of loving extravagantly, I was put to the test. Chuck has a large radio-controlled model airplane that has been a part of his life for nearly forty years—he started building it when he was eight and finally finished it twenty years later. We have painstakingly moved it from house to house. He has too much of himself invested in it to risk flying it. With a five-foot wingspan, you cannot just tuck it anyplace. In our current home, the now-famous airplane has its own special location complete with a spotlight. However, for ten years it hung in our former house near the peak of the cathedral ceiling in the family room—directly over my desk, the place where I wrote uplifting and encouraging Christian books.

The plane is bright red with Red Baron-like decals. While I'd prefer to have the plane in the garage, I have accepted it as a conversation piece—and you can be sure it is—because it is important to Chuck.

One day, shortly after I had committed to love Chuck extravagantly, he took the airplane to a model airplane show. He spent hours cleaning off the accumulated dust that had firmly attached itself to every surface. The plane was very popular at the show, and he discovered how valuable it really was. Before he put it back on its hook, he wanted to protect it, so he covered the body and wings with plastic dry cleaning bags with "Comet Cleaners" clearly visible in yellow and black.

I like my home to look like a showplace; just *having* the airplane there is an act of compromise and love. Having it covered with baggy dry-cleaning bags with words on them went too far. "I'll never be able to entertain again," I wailed to him. After my outburst—which I knew was an overreaction —I went outside and trimmed my roses. As I took a deep breath, "love extravagantly" came to mind. Does it really matter if the airplane has a bag over it? What is more important: that my husband is happy or that I have a lovely home? Hmm . . . that was tough. "Love extravagantly," I told myself. I came back in and apologized—ready to accept the dry-cleaning bags. Meanwhile, he had decided that I was right and it really was ugly. He had taken the plane down, removed the dry cleaning bags, and was replacing them with clear plastic wrap that clings tightly to every curve and doesn't even show!

While your story may be different and probably doesn't include a model airplane, chances are that you too need to adopt my personal mission: not cautious love but extravagant, not to get but to give. What changes do you need to make to love your spouse extravagantly?

As I continue to speak on the message of *You've Got What It Takes*, I've found that the need for the Love Extravagantly principle is universal. What had begun as a small part of my previous book has grown into a book of its own. On the following pages you will see snapshots of modern marriages. I see that, today, many of us find ourselves in messy marriage situations—you'll read about some of them in this book—but because these conditions are not what our parents and grandparents faced, we do not know how to deal with them. There is no specific set of rules that works for all marriages anymore. Most of today's marriages have no script to follow that tells them what to do in a specific situation—making them unscripted. While no one answer works for everyone, we can all follow the biblical Love Extravagantly principle. When we stop and look at our current marriage predicaments with a "not to get, but to give" attitude, we can create a fresh script based on biblical truth for the modern marriage. Regardless of what type of modern marriage you have, the examples found on the following pages will give you practical solutions for today that can apply to your own marriage and produce similar results. With all the changes in today's family structure, couples need something more than just love to make their marriages work. They need to love extravagantly!

Introduction

Marriage: A New Script

Each morning, I drag my body out of bed and after a brief stop in the bathroom, I head for the kitchen. Harley and Triumph, our schnauzer children, bound down the stairs and head for the back door where they wait for me to tell them to go outside. At my command they squeeze through the little space, fighting over who will get outside first—as if there will be some new and exciting thing that was not there the day before. Lacking their enthusiasm for morning, I trudge back into the kitchen, fill the teakettle, and place it on the stove.

I step out the front door where I dump yesterday's coffee grounds out of the French press and onto the plants. I rinse it, and add three scoops of fresh coffee—on weekends I grind fresh beans. I select one of my husband's favorite mugs bearing the likeness of a schnauzer. For myself, I choose a tall porcelain cup, open the package of my favorite tea, and place the bag in the cup.

When the coffee is ready, I fill Chuck's cup, add some cream, and pour the rest of the coffee into a thermal carafe. With his coffee cup in one hand and my tea in the other, I head back up the stairs to the bathroom. By now Chuck is in the shower. I hand his coffee in to him. Through the sound of the spray I hear, "Thanks, Rabbit."

While he showers, I wash my face, put in my contacts, and apply my makeup. As he dresses, I go back down to the kitchen and cook his breakfast—a fresh, hot Belgian waffle with bacon or sausage. We eat together while flipping through the selection of morning shows in search of news, and carrying on as much conversation as the early hour allows. After rubbing my shoulders in thanks, Chuck leaves for work. I do the dishes. Then I get dressed, lock up the house, and go to work.

If we were an average American family—if there were such a thing—this scene is what would happen each morning at your house too! We'd all be following the same script.

Equilibrium: A Script that Works

Our morning ritual is what works for us. It is part of the balance that has made our marriage successful over the last twenty-two years. In our script—the unwritten rules of our marriage—Chuck says he'll hurt himself shaving if he doesn't have coffee first thing in the morning. I am not caffeine dependent, so I bring it to him. His stomach and mind need good fuel to function effectively. I like to cook, so I make him what he likes—even though many days I make eggs for myself. Chuck jokes that he likes his breakfast so much he has chosen John 21:12 as his life verse: "Jesus said to them, 'Come and eat breakfast'" (NKJV).

My sister and her husband have been married thirty-plus years. A few years ago I visited them for five days. As I observed their life together, I was struck by how different it was from my marriage. Randy makes coffee for both of them while Lauren is still in bed. If breakfast is made, Randy usually does it. Our morning routines are merely a sampling of the differences in our marriages. Their marriage is different, but it is also successful. Over the years their marriage has written its own script that works for them with their personalities and their place in life.

After observing my sister's marriage, I thought about my parents. They had been married forty-nine years when my father died. When I stayed in their home and traveled with them, I saw their relationship in action. Their marriage had its own characteristics; they created their own script that worked for them. My father took care of every little need for my mother to the point that if she wanted to call me, he dialed the phone, said hello, and then handed the phone off to her. I'd feel suffocated under such circumstances. She felt pampered and special and without him has had to learn to use her cell phone and send faxes on her own—not to mention doing grocery shopping and cooking her own meals.

When my friend Eva Marie read about my morning routine, she said, "If I got up and made a waffle for Dennis, he would think I had charged too much on one of my credit cards and was trying to soften the blow. Or perhaps that I wrecked the car! In fact, in my house, I rarely cook! We eat what we can, when we can! For us, it works . . . especially now that there are only the two of us."

Each of our marriages is different, yet each has stood the test of time—each is successful. Over the years, we have each developed our own balance. We have created what I like to call an equilibrium that works for each individual couple. While this parity brings about a marriage with which each couple is happy, we could not trade places and expect the same procedures or rituals to work for the other couples as each union is made up of different factors. What works for Chuck and me will not automatically have the same results in your marriage. Your marriage needs its own equilibrium—its own script.

When my sister and her husband visited us and watched our marriage script play out, I'd guess that my sister wouldn't want to change places with me. Both Lauren and Chuck would be waiting for someone to bring them their coffee! While Chuck and I have created an equilibrium that works for us, I know most of my friends wouldn't want my marriage either!

The Modern Marriage

So, if I have a marriage no one would want to replicate, why am I writing a book on marriage? I am writing this not because I am an expert, not because I have the model or perfect marriage, and not because I have all the answers. I am writing because I realize that there is no perfect marriage, no average American family, and no single script that works for everyone.

I am writing because I understand that each union brings to the table different needs, expectations, backgrounds, and personalities that make every marriage unique.[1] As such, no one book or one formula will work for everyone. Each couple needs to find their own equilibrium—their own script.

My marriage has some specific characteristics that make it different from many of my friends' marriages. Yet, it also has traits that I find are like so many other marriages today. In my marriage, and possibly yours as well, little resembles what was modeled in my youth as the ideal marriage. When I was growing up there was a set script; television programs led us to believe that all marriages fit a certain mold. Today, many churches still function as if this is the script everyone follows. This unwritten set of rules is what I define as the traditional marriage: first marriage for both spouses. Husband goes off to work every day and is the sole breadwinner. His job is secure and he works for the same company all his life. He is the leader, the disciplinarian (remember "Wait 'til your father gets home"?), and the decision maker in the family. Wife stays home and takes care of the children and her husband. She is sweet, gracious, and agreeable to whatever her husband suggests. I call this family the "Ozzie-and-Harriet model," named for the perfect television family of the fifties and sixties. If you are younger, you might relate more to television families such as the Huxtables from *The Cosby Show* and the Seavers from *Growing Pains*. Every generation has its own version of the model family—a recent family model that television offers would be the Camden family from *7th Heaven*.

My friend Kim says, "I remember watching my parents' Ozzie-and-Harriet marriage, and while I respected them, I did not want to follow my mother's script for my life! As it turns out, our lives are very different. But we are both happy. However, I can't figure out how my mother fills her days now!"

Those of us who do not fit the Ozzie-and-Harriet script have what I call a modern marriage. This script may include a wide variety of scenes:

- A marriage where both spouses work and are income-producing. They may work outside the home or have a home-based business, but they both produce income—perhaps the woman makes more than her husband does or he works for her.
- A marriage that is a second or third marriage for one or both

spouses. There may be ex-spouse problems or stepchildren that factor into the marriage.
- A marriage where the couple has chosen to be childless.
- A "commuter marriage" where spouses may have to live apart for a period of time due to career changes or a need to care for an aging parent.
- A marriage in which there is something as subtle as the wife having the stronger personality.

Because each marriage is unique, these are just a sampling of the situations that may constitute the modern marriage—one for which there is no set script.

As an author, books are my world. When I review Christian books on marriage, I find many of them assume that marriages are still following the Ozzie-and-Harriet script. While this standard script, the traditional marriage, is a blessed way to live, looking at my marriage and those of my friends, I find that this model is rare today. For many of us, the principles and ideals outlined in the many excellent books available on marriage do not apply.

If, like me, you have read some of these books and felt frustrated because they seem so out of touch with the reality of your household, this book is for you. Since there are many wonderful books out there that address the basics of a traditional marriage, I have chosen to address those of us who feel left out. This book will look at a cross section of unique marriage situations—those problems that many of our parents didn't have to face—and help you find the equilibrium that is right for your particular set of circumstances. As there is no longer a set script that we all follow in our marriages, there is no way to address every possible scene being played out on the stage of your house. However, as you read the variety of possible marriage scripts on the following pages, you will find many situations that are similar to yours and you will be able to glean from the principles presented.

I have what I call a modern marriage, but because I had been modeled a traditional marriage as a child, I had "traditional" expectations of my own marriage. I thought I was supposed to follow this traditional script, but I could not make my modern marriage fit the traditional script. I realized that I was trying to attain an unrealistic image. So I had to make adjustments in my expectations of what I thought my marriage would be, but there was no guide for me as to how to make my modern marriage work.

As a licensed Professional Clinical Counselor specializing in marriage, my husband, Chuck, often asks the couple in his office to paint a word picture of their childhood model of marriage. He asks them to use an analogy of a television show, a fairy tale, or storybook that reflects their view of marriage. The response is often something like "Father Knows Best," "Ozzie and Harriet," "Leave It to Beaver," or "Cinderella." Next he asks them, "Is that what you expect from your marriage today? Is that what you really want from your marriage?" After a pause in which the lights go on, the couple usually realizes they have unconsciously tried to script their real-life, modern marriage into a fairy tale "happily-ever-after" story. But this only results in fighting and disagreements. Once the couple is able to acknowledge that their expectations are unrealistic—and often not even really what they want today—they can accept where they are and build from there.

When discussing this book with my friend Jan, she said, "I wish there was a book like this available fifteen years ago. I might still be married today. I tried so hard to be Harriet, but that was just not me. My expectations were unrealistic. I was the strong personality. I tried so hard to be sweet and submissive, to bake cookies and have dinner ready on time. I thought I was the only one who struggled with what I perceived as the right way. But, that was the script I'd seen played out in my parents' home. It was all I knew to do."

As you read the scenarios in the following chapters, you will see that you are not alone—as Jan thought she was. You will see that other couples have problems too. But, most importantly, you will see that when you care enough to apply the principle of "Love Extravagantly"— loving as Christ did, not to get but to give—most of the problems you face can be solved.

A few years ago, when I first began to develop these ideas, I shared them with my mother. She could see that I definitely had a modern marriage. I owned my own business when I got married. I have always worked outside the home, and I have always expected to work—in fact, I look forward to it. At many phases of our marriage, I have been the primary breadwinner.

My husband was married briefly before we met. While he is my first, and only, husband, I am his second wife. After twenty-two years of marriage, we have still never felt ready to have children—we are childless by choice. I use my maiden name professionally and my married name privately. I am known as Marita Littauer and my husband as Chuck Noon. Clearly we have a modern marriage; we do not fit the Ozzie-and-Harriet model.

As I look around, I see the unscripted, modern marriage everywhere. As I began to develop these ideas, my mother proudly proclaimed that she had a "traditional marriage." I chuckled. "How do you figure?" I asked. "You work outside the home. You are the primary breadwinner. And your husband worked for you."

"Oh," she replied, "I guess I was thinking of when you kids were young."

Yes, my mother was a true stay-at-home mom when I was young and my dad the only breadwinner. They had the usual script for their day. But in their later years of marriage that all changed. They had to create a new equilibrium that worked for their changed circumstances.

My sister is more traditional in that she has three sons and has made parenting her priority. Neither she nor her husband had been married before. She was twenty and he was twenty-six when they got married. However, with her strong personality, she has almost always had some type of enterprise going on. Her husband is more low-key; he owns his own business and she has often worked with him in the store. She has had a real estate license for twenty-five years, managed a thriving real estate business for a major broker in her town, and remains active in the real estate market today. She has a sharp business mind and does bookkeeping and management consulting for several small businesses. She does newsletter design and editing for a few clients, including me. And now that her youngest is out of the house and in college, and the other boys are on their own, she has gotten back into speaking and writing as she did before her children were born.

My brother married later in life. He was thirty-five. It is his first marriage, but his wife had been married briefly before. She was twenty-eight. They met at work, but when they got married, company policy prevented them from working together. She found another job. When they had their first child, she went back to work for a while but hated leaving the baby in day care. Now, they are the closest to the standard script of anyone in our family. By the time this book is off the press, they will have two children and she has been blessed to be a stay-at-home mom for several years.

That is my family. What about my friends? Here is a sampling of the variety of marriages we find today:

Dianne and Mark have been married fourteen years. It is a first marriage for both. They were each in their early thirties when they got married. They worked together in the television news business. Their first child was born shortly after their first anniversary and their second less than two years later. Their jobs required lots of late nights—a schedule that is not conducive to parenting. It quickly became clear that one of them had to make a change. Since Dianne was the news anchor and Mark the reporter, he left network news to start his own consulting business. Dianne remained the primary breadwinner for many years. When Mark's business was doing well and their kids were nine and eleven, Dianne left the nightly news for midday talk radio. With her name recognition, she was offered enough money for fewer hours to make the switch. After a few months on the air, another change was made. The station offered Mark a cohost position with Dianne and they are now working together at the radio station and working together to keep Mark's consulting business going.

Ann and Gerry have been married twenty-two years. They own a business together. They each have their own skills that have made the business a success. But they both also have different ideas about how the business should be run. While these differences have helped, they have also been a major source of stress in their marriage. It is Ann's third marriage, and she has three grown children from her first marriage. It is Gerry's second marriage, and he has no children—although he has been like a father to Ann's children as the oldest was a teenager when they got married. Like Chuck and me, and my brother and his wife, Ann has the stronger personality and Gerry is content to be in the background.

Trish and Pat have been married nearly twenty years. They have two young children. Both Trish and Pat were Olympic athletes and, in fact, met in Seoul, Korea at the 1988 Olympics. Pat has a degree in finance and, after his career as a professional runner, he now works for a major homebuilder. Trish currently holds the world record in the high jump for women in her age range. Much of her life has been consumed with track and field activities and, while Pat is the major breadwinner, Trish works as a track coach with both the local high schools and university.

These are some of the couples in my life. Do you see any consistency? They are all different, no one script works for all of them—that is why I like to think of the modern marriage as unscripted. Look around. I believe you will find a similar variety of circumstances in the marriages that surround you. The patterns we observed in our youth are no longer valid for many of us. The roles the media portrayed back then are no longer relevant for most of us today. The expectations society formerly placed on our marriages aren't realistic anymore. So where are we to look for help, guidance, and answers to the unique situations of the modern marriage—the one that has no set script?

How to Use This Book

This book is as unique and modern as the marriages I hope to help. Rather than outline a specific script of success for every marriage to follow, it recognizes the premise that each marriage is unique—there is no longer an average American family. While all marriages are different, many do face similar problems and difficulties. In the following pages you will find a collection of real-life scenarios—which I've called "The Issue." Gathered through e-mail and the Internet, these scenarios have also been reviewed by real-life couples worldwide. Those who have faced something similar in their marriages have offered "peer" insights as to how they got through the situation and found their own equilibrium. These insights are presented with the contributors' first names only. In most cases their real names are used; however, some have asked that their identity be protected. Some of these peers have input in only one chapter, others have commented in several—depending on their personal experience.

Additionally, therapists and other experts have given advice based on their professional experience and what they have seen work in similar situations. To make their contributions easy to identify, the "professional" insights are identified by the use of their first and last names and title. Appendix C, at the end of the book, is a directory of these professionals. Please review it for more information on them and their ministries or practices.

As a writer, a personality expert, and someone with a burden for the modern marriage, I am bringing the issues, the peer insights, and the professional advice together and adding the input on the personality complications. (I highly recommend that you review or study the appendix on Personality Types. I will be referring to them throughout the book.) While his fingers seldom touched the keyboard, my husband, Chuck Noon, has added his opinion—mostly through our dinner conversation and rollerblading excursions.

The combined advice from the peers and professionals is under the heading "The Insights."

At the end of each chapter you will find activities—called "The Interactions"—to assist you in putting the teaching into practice. If you were actually visiting a counselor, these activities would be the homework you would be asked to do before returning for the next session.

While all the scenarios are different, they have been grouped under the following headings: Personal, Career, Financial, Ex-spouse, and Stepfamily. In my marriage, most of our difficulties revolve around the career and financial areas. So, as a reader, I would read those parts but skip the part on stepfamily issues, which does not apply to me. Many of my friends would spend most of their time in the ex-spouse and stepfamily areas.

Because this book is designed in such a way that you are encouraged to hopscotch through it—reading the parts that apply to you—some of the concepts are presented more than once. Insights, too, may be similar in several situations as concepts are repeated in the appropriate settings.

Chuck and I recommend that every couple use the communication exercise found in appendix C. It will be helpful for virtually every scenario offered in this book. While certain personality types—especially the Powerful Cholerics and the Peaceful Phlegmatics—are apt to be resistant to this type of work, it should only take about fifteen to twenty minutes a day (or an hour each week). It always pays big dividends. It is referred to in various chapters as The Couple's Communication Exercise.

Browse the table of contents. By reading the scenarios that most closely fit your unique situation, you will gain insight, guidance, and advice specifically applicable to you, allowing you and your spouse to create an equilibrium that works for your marriage. Write your own script!

PART 1
PERSONAL ISSUES

One

The Fire's Gone Out

Personality Differences, Physical Relationship

The Issue

Todd is a Peaceful Phlegmatic and a schoolteacher. Erica is a Powerful Choleric, although most of her life she has functioned in her role as a Perfect Melancholy—her secondary personality. Todd and Erica were high school sweethearts and married young. Todd settled into being the breadwinner, while Erica managed the home. Erica became pregnant with their first child on their honeymoon. Two more children quickly followed. Erica was a good mother and used her natural abilities to manage the family in an enviable manner.

When the youngest reached high school, Erica found she had more time on her hands. She began taking classes in real estate, and within two years she had become the top producer in her area.

As she competed in the business world, she adopted the characteristics of other professionals. She developed her Powerful Choleric personality and took on the fast-talking, multitasking, cell-phone-packing style so dominant in our culture. The money rolled in.

Meanwhile, Todd labored away in the public schools, feeling unappreciated and underpaid. In comparison, his modest salary seemed inferior to Erica's commissioned sales income.

In social settings Todd went from respected educator and leader of a beautiful family to "Aren't you Erica's husband?" Todd felt he had lost his role as provider and leader of the family.

All of this took a toll on their sex life. Erica confided in her best friend saying, "Todd hasn't touched me in months." Todd found the "new Erica" threatening and unappealing. As he withdrew and sulked, Erica found him increasingly unattractive.

There are confident men at Erica's office, and there are pretty young teachers at Todd's school. A potential crisis!

The Insights

Todd and Erica are at the place where many couples find themselves. They have had a stable marriage for years, yet now find their marriage struggling. Kris commented,

> This is such a typical twist in a marriage. Pete and I are going through a somewhat similar situation. Although I haven't yet finished my education for a new role in life, I see Pete winding down after a successful career and looking for home time—which is all I ever had!

Chuck has frequently seen this dynamic when working with post-retirement military couples. For twenty years the wife supported the career of the husband, moving every two or three years. After retirement the wife says, "Now it is my time." But it is hard for the "old soldier" to change.

We often see a marriage that has appeared to be good and solid for fifteen to twenty-five years suddenly crumble when the family roles shift. People on the outside wonder what happened. In reality, rather than living the happy marriage everyone thought they had, they had developed a lifestyle in which they had grown comfortable. As we see in our case-history couple, Todd and Erica's relationship had the predictability of Ozzie-and-Harriet. They had developed an equilibrium that gave them a sense of stability and balance.

As a Peaceful Phlegmatic, we can assume that Todd was comfortable with the routine his home life had taken on. However, as a Powerful Choleric with some Perfect Melancholy, Erica was ready for a change. She was ready to spread her wings and develop her gifts outside of her role as a wife and mother. Anytime a relationship undergoes such a major shift in the equilibrium, there are bound to be problems that arise during the adjustment period.

While there are many aspects of the relationship that could be discussed, several are well covered in other chapters. If this scenario relates to your situation, please be sure to read the following chapters, as much of their content also will apply: "Lack of Time Together," "Merging Finances," and "Rocky Roads." These chapters address issues such as finding one's self-worth in God rather than employment, combining incomes, and creating quality time together. Here we cover the two issues that are applicable to Todd and Erica: their personality differences and their physical relationship.

Personality Differences

Reprioritize Your Life

Because Erica made the changes, she is the one whose actions knocked the equilibrium out of balance in the marriage. She will need to put in the most effort to help establish a new center. In response to this situation, Roseanne P. Elling, LPC, says,

> This marriage needs some reprioritizing, especially on the part of Erica. She may have to choose her marriage ("us") over her career ("me") at times.

We know Erica is a Powerful Choleric, though these traits had taken a back seat during her prime mothering years. As such, we assume her need for leadership, control, and recognition have been boiling below the surface, waiting to get out for many years. Consequently, telling her to quit her job and go back to being a full-time mom would only solve the problem on the outside—leaving Erica champing at the bit.

For Erica, real estate is a good option as it allows flexibility to be available when her youngest son needs her. Meeting her needs without ignoring her husband's, is Erica's struggle.

If Erica were to come to her for counsel, Dr. Ruth Kopp says,

> First, I would ask Erica what she wants. Does she want to be right, to be vindicated, to have me agree that she is entitled to her career success? Or does she want her marriage revitalized and a right relationship with her husband? If she wants to be "right" there is no real hope for the marriage.

While the scenario doesn't state a Christian commitment, we can assume both Todd and Erica are Christians. As such, they know that divorce is never a part of God's perfect plan, and they desire to make their marriage work. Both will need to make some changes, both will need to be willing to love extravagantly—not to get, but to give.

Before Todd and Erica can look at the presenting problem—"He hasn't touched me in months"—they need to address their relationship. Shellie Arnold has a lay ministry promoting intimacy in couples. She states,

> Intimacy is what happens when our hearts, emotions, minds, and spirits are functioning properly, with or without sex. Todd and Erica's sex life is suffering because their intimate life is suffering.

Recognize Personality Requirements

To begin to build their relationship back up, each needs to gain an understanding of their personalities and the emotional needs that accompany the way God created them. Victoria Jackson, MSW, recommends that Erica and Todd,

> Consider studying the personality styles each of you are and note how you have changed since the beginning of marriage. Celebrate the differences. View it as an exciting aspect of your relationship.

For strong women who are married to men who have quieter personalities, the contrast seems exaggerated as society, and especially the church, expects that the man is the leader and the woman the follower. When this is not the way we are wired, as in the case of Erica and Todd, we women need to put forth the extra effort to understand and lift up our husband.

Dr. Ruth Kopp, who faces a similar personality combination in her own marriage says,

> The Powerful Choleric will usually be the one to take the initiative in learning to "speak Peaceful Phlegmatic" and will need to be willing to initiate change and make the majority of changes.

Diane agrees with Dr. Kopp.

> As someone who is in the "reverse" role in later married life, I can relate to the upset in balance. I believe it's incumbent on the wife to try and ensure that her husband is feeling needed and wanted by her. Oftentimes, we appear so self-sufficient that our husbands think they don't have anything to give us anymore and that they are not our number-one priority (and often, they're not). Peaceful Phlegmatics don't realize that, as they withdraw, they become more annoying to the Powerful Choleric and less attractive, perpetuating a downward cycle. My experience is that the wife must go out of her way to assure her husband that she still values him.

Being willing to take this first step is where the love extravagantly concept becomes important.

Chuck and I have a similar personality combination in that I am more the up-front person, more the leader. He is content in the background and shuns the spotlight. I long for social activity and a large network of friends. He is happy with one or two friendships that have developed over decades. Like Erica, I am in the business world. Chuck and Todd are not. Chuck as a therapist and Todd as a teacher, function in the world of the arts and sciences. I have had to learn to adjust to his needs. I used to come home in what Chuck called "boss mode"—with my Powerful Choleric traits dominant. He often had to remind me that he was not one of my employees. This side of me highlighted my less attractive traits that were particularly unattractive to Chuck.

Meet Emotional Needs

Because I love Chuck and want to make our marriage work and because I understand our personality differences, I have been able to modify my behavior—especially when I am with him.

I have made a conscious decision to love Chuck extravagantly, to make changes in my approach that boost Chuck and his self-esteem.

When Nance married my Uncle Ron, she was already successful as a real estate agent. However, as a popular radio personality, he was used to acclaim. I remember her saying that when she is with him, she views her job as carrying the spotlight and shining it on him. It takes a secure woman to be willing to set aside her success and/or fame to shine the spotlight on her husband; this is exactly what Erica needs to do.

Make Necessary Adjustments

So, first I'd encourage Erica to understand Todd's Peaceful Phlegmatic Personality (see app. A). Erica can love him extravagantly by making adjustments to minimize the upheaval and change her career has brought into his life. She can draw upon her Perfect Melancholy strengths when she is with him, tone down her voice, and maintain the order at home to which he is accustomed. Roseanne Elling tells of some friends of hers who are in a similar situation, but have learned what the other needs:

> The Powerful Choleric wife pays attention to some little things, such as how her Peaceful Phlegmatic husband likes the towels in the bathroom folded. She takes time to do the things she knows are important to him. Although she is busy and is a top performer in her field, her attention to his desires makes him feel that he is important to her.

Both in private and in public, any woman in Erica's place needs to shine the spotlight on her husband. This is apt to take some real effort on her part, but if her true desire is to love him extravagantly, through the power of the Holy Spirit, she can do it. The difficulty is that Powerful Cholerics respect strength. After being out in the business community with high visibility men whose activities command respect, a Peaceful Phlegmatic husband may look dull and boring—not strong.

Melanie Wilson suggests that if Todd were to share with Erica how he feels about making a difference in the lives of his students, despite his comparatively low salary, Erica may view him in a new perspective. Erica needs to be able to feel proud of Todd and the work he does, his achievements and accomplishments.

In making the attitude adjustment to feel proud of her husband, Ruth Kopp says,

> I'm a Powerful Choleric. My husband's Perfect Melancholy tendencies slow me down and I can choose to be impatient with them and brush them aside (and end up being sorry!), or I can see that God has put him in my life precisely to slow me down and make me think! When I remember to check with him before making business decisions, I make better decisions, and we are a team.

Reflecting on her friends' situation, Roseanne Elling says,

> She is very proud of what he does and talks about it, much more than she talks about her own work in social situations. I believe she is comfortable with herself and gets enough acclaim for her success at work, so she doesn't feel like she's competing when she's at home or out socially. Her admiration of her Peaceful Phlegmatic husband's character and his personal job success, although it is very different than hers, is obvious to all who are around them. He feels respected by her.

While Erica may need to be the one to take the first step, both will need to make some adjustments to save their marriage. Georgia Shaffer advises,

Erica and Todd need to be cautious and affirm each other rather than looking for affirmation in the people at work. It is so easy to be pulled in by the encouragement and compliments of those who don't have to live with us week in and week out. Many people don't plan to have affairs, but before they know it they are emotionally swept away by the steady dose of attention and compliments.

In understanding that as a Powerful Choleric Erica needs appreciation for all she does, Todd can make new efforts at appreciating and admiring her skills and abilities—this is where love extravagantly will come into play for him.

Andrea Golzmane, MA, LMFT, says,

> We all resist change, especially when the relationship itself changes. The sign of a healthy marriage is a spouse's willingness to be flexible, to "step out of the box," and be creative.

Marj, one of our peer advisors, is an attorney with a background in real estate. She is a Powerful Choleric married to a Peaceful Phlegmatic. From her experience, Marj suggests the following:

> Erica deserves to spread her wings and fly, especially after years of tending children and home, but she cannot do so at the expense of her marriage. She needs to watch carefully the time she gives her husband and make sure that he gets a fair dose of quality time.
>
> Todd needs to be supportive of his wife. She gave up "flying" for years to tend to the family and home. He needs to get involved with her job. He will find that there is a lot to do, and that his help will be greatly appreciated by his wife. They will then be more of a team, and can enjoy the fruits of their labor together. When Todd is introduced as "Erica's husband," Erica can proudly say that without Todd, she could not have done it (rather than that her success came in spite of him.)
>
> His help could include going with her to open houses. Dur-

ing times when no one is there, they can be together. When many people are there, he can be of assistance answering questions, being friendly, etc.

As Erica and Todd begin to understand each other's personality and make adjustments in their relationship accordingly, they will begin to find each other more appealing. In reviewing the situation, we can see that they have grown apart; Todd feels set aside as the head of the house and Erica feels unwanted as a woman.

Before addressing the issues of sex, Roseanne Elling reminds them that they are a team: "It's very difficult to feel romantic when you're competing."

Physical Relationship

Erica has complained that Todd has not "touched her in months." As we have seen, their relationship needs work before they even look at the sexual issues. Once they learn to meet each other's differing emotional needs, the sex issues may take care of themselves. As they rediscover each other and make an effort to enjoy one another again, they are creating an environment of affection. In his book *His Needs, Her Needs*, Willard Harley states, "Affection is the environment of the marriage and sex is the special event."[1] Everything we have discussed up to this point is about creating that environment. Now, on to the special event.

Here both spouses can do things spiritually, physically, and emotionally to set the stage for the "special event," but again, the wife can lead in this area. Diane addresses this beautifully.

> Our husbands also need to know that we desire them. We can purpose in our hearts to create romantic interludes with our husbands. Be playful, soft, vulnerable. Bottom line—the relationship between husband and wife is ultimately far more valuable than a successful career. If we take as much time to cultivate this mentality with our husbands as we do in being successful, we can experience the greatest success in both arenas!

I love her idea of using our success mindset to be successful in this aspect of our lives as well. We Powerful Choleric women love a good challenge. Making sex a special event after a damaged relationship will be a challenge, but one that can be conquered. It will be worth the effort!

Start with Prayer

The place for Erica to start is with prayer. She needs to pray for an attitude adjustment so she will be willing to take the physical and emotional steps to improve their sex life. In responding to Erica's situation, Suzy offered the following:

> Whenever I have found my husband "unappealing," I have done two things. First, I pray about my sex life. I know this sounds simple, but many times we do not ask God for help. I started praying about my sexual experience when my husband went through a depression many years ago, and he didn't seem to be the man I married. Whew! If God doesn't honor our prayers! He created sex and knows how to make it what it was intended to be! The next thing I did was try to recreate the things that sexually attracted me to my husband in the first place. We love to workout together, so we found time to play together by swimming, running, and playing tennis. After that, I saw him in a whole different light.

Shellie Arnold advises further:

> In the Garden of Eden, before sin entered the world and Adam and Eve's marriage, Scripture tells us, "And the man and his wife were both naked and were not embarrassed or ashamed in each other's presence" (Gen. 2:25 AMP). Todd and Erica will have to work to strip the stress and persona of the day away and get reconnected physically. God loves to help lovemaking become more fruitful and enjoyable for His children. After all, it was His idea and His plan in the first place.

Prayer is the best place to start. In her book *The Power of a Praying Wife,* Stormie Omartian suggests the following prayer:

> Lord, bless my husband's sexuality and make it an area of great fulfillment for him. Restore what needs to be restored, balance what needs to be balanced. Protect us from apathy, disappointment, criticism, busyness, unforgiveness, deadness, or disinterest. I pray that we make time for one another, communicate our true feelings openly, and remain sensitive to each other's needs.[2]

Have Realistic Expectations

It may be helpful for Erica to realize that at this phase of life, sex is probably not ever going to be what it was on the honeymoon. After reading Erica and Todd's situation, a peer advisor, Mallory, wrote,

> Sex, now let me think . . . what was that like? A few years ago I went to my dentist—a 100 percent Popular Sanguine woman. While waiting I skimmed *Parade Magazine* and read its decade report on the sex profile of Americans. When my dentist's hand was out of my mouth, I shared what I had read with her. It said the middle-aged group had sex seven times a month—we both died laughing . . . wondering who did it that many times when we were all working and exhausted and could care less? Somehow the pace of living has us fall into bed together, hug, snuggle, and fall asleep. . . . However, I can honestly say that our relationship is much better when we *do* have sex! It really does bring a sense of intimacy like nothing else does.

Like Erica and Todd, Cassie's marriage is in a role reversal stage as well. She reports,

> Lovemaking is less frequent, but definitely more tender. When we do make love, it generally starts out slower and builds. In this period of life, I have found that the danger for older couples, even

with intimate conversation and sharing, can be feeling more like brothers and sisters than lovers. This is another reason to continue to seek a healthy and satisfying relationship.

Fan the Flame

Yes, sex does change in the different phases of a couple's life, but it can be fanned into a flame again. There are many nights when falling into bed together, hugging, snuggling, and falling asleep is the best we can do. Yet, when we are on vacation, the statistics are totally different. During a week in St. Thomas we walked hand-in-hand on the beach. We went snorkeling. We had fun dinners together. We sat on the balcony of our room and watched the sunset. Without the stresses and cares of daily life, we rediscovered a honeymoon quality of romance. We have found similar results at a nearby bed and breakfast and at a friend's borrowed mountain cabin.

Order Your Priorities

When Chuck works with couples, he coaches them to begin looking at long and short-term priorities. When asked, most of us would order our priorities: God, spouse, children, and so on. Yet on a day-to-day basis our lives are filled with short-term trivia. If the gas gauge on the car says empty, we put gas in the car now or it will grind to a stop. Often we go days, weeks, or even years without putting any gas into our marriage. Because the intimate relationship can wait, it never comes up as a priority unless we truly make it one.

Addressing the importance of making the sexual relationship a priority, Stormie Omartian writes,

> After twenty years of praying with women about their failing, struggling, unfulfilling, or dead marriages, I've observed that frequently the sexual relationship is a low priority. It isn't that the wife cares nothing about that part of her life. It's that there are so many other things screaming for her attention, such as raising children, work, finances, managing a home, emotional

stress, exhaustion, sickness, and marital strife. In the wife's juggling of priorities, sex can end up at the bottom of her list. Some women allow week after week, month after month, six months a year to go by without having sexual relations with their husbands for one reason or another. When disaster hits, they are surprised.[3]

Run Away Together

Couples in Erica and Todd's place need to take some time away to have fun and focus on each other. Evelyn Davison is known as the "Christian Dr. Ruth" in Austin, Texas where her daily radio program "LoveTalk" airs. She offers this advice:

> When the passion flickers low, take a day or weekend off to spend time together without phones or beepers. Do something that was fun when you first got married. Forget the kids at school and the clients at the office. After the physical fun activity (not sexual), separate for at least an hour and write out a "things I have always loved about you" list. Then meet again somewhere with an atmosphere conducive to conversation like a coffeehouse or a bluff overlooking the city and take turns sharing the list of "I love yous." This can help move you to compassion for the needs of each other. The surprise comes when the passion returns. It may not be as hot as it was on the honeymoon sexual encounter, but it should be lively!

If finances or responsibilities dictate that a week in the Caribbean is not feasible, look for other options. Perhaps friends have a cabin in the mountains that can provide the same type of getaway—away from the cares of the world and into the world of each other. If your situation is similar to Erica and Todd, you may need to start with more than a day—a full weekend—together or, better yet, a week.

After an extended period of time away from everyday life to reconnect—emotionally, physically, and spiritually—Todd and Erica will need to make specific plans to keep the flame fanned once they are back into their routine at home. Creative time together is discussed more completely in the chapter "Lack of Time Together."

Whether or not they are on a "date," Chuck suggests that Erica leave the business persona at the office. When she comes home, she needs to make a conscious effort to switch into her role of wife and mother. This may involve turning off the cell phone, taking off the "gold jacket," and mentally slowing down. Something as simple as a change of clothing can impact a mental shift.

Dress the Set

While clothing can be important, the rest of our surroundings can be as well. Chuck's undergraduate degree is in motion picture production. From this background he suggests that Todd and Erica "dress the set," meaning to make their bedroom a place conducive to making love. When couples come to Chuck with sexual problems in their marriage, he has learned to ask, "Do you have an ironing board and a basket of laundry in the bedroom?" More often than not, the answer is yes. There may be a computer on a desk next to the bed or other paraphernalia that has nothing to do with what goes on in a bedroom. While household space may cause limitations for some couples, as much as possible prepare the bedroom for a romantic interlude.

I remember hearing my mother speak on the topic of marriage when I was a teenager. She asked the women in her audience, "If your husband was going to have an affair today, while you are here at this conference, would he do it in your bedroom in the condition you left it this morning?" An audible gasp was heard throughout the crowd as most left an unmade bed, baskets of laundry, an ironing board, and more cluttering the bedroom. The point, of course, was not to prepare the bedroom for your husband to have an affair with another woman, but to keep it in a condition where he will want to have one with you!

Stir the Embers

As Erica takes steps to invite Todd to make love, he, too, needs to make Erica feel needed and feminine. Chuck suggests that Todd purchase feminine lingerie and perfume for her. Sweep her off her feet!

As Erica and Todd love each other with extravagance, setting aside what is fair and doing what is right for their marriage, they will find that the fire has not gone out completely. There are embers that can be stirred and brought back to life. Roseanne Elling says,

> Couples mistakenly believe that the fire of the honeymoon continues to roar on its own. The truth is that it burns inconsistently, sometimes flaring up, sometimes burning steadily, and sometimes waning into mere embers. It's up to both partners to keep the fire burning, and it takes effort!

The Interactions

For couples in a similar situation to Todd and Erica, Chuck would assign the following "homework" assignment:

1. Both husband and wife need to alternate days as the initiator of intimacy. Relationships tend to fall into a pursuer/distancer dynamic. The longer that each member of the couple remains in the same role, the further the couple tends to grow apart. By reversing roles frequently, the couple grows together. The husband might take odd days with the wife taking the even ones. Being the pursuer means initiating intimacy with touch, kisses, hugs, saying "I love you," etc.
2. The husband should buy, gift wrap, and present intimate attire that is sexy, yet tasteful. He should rehearse the compliments he will offer the wife when she is wearing his selection that will make her know he finds her attractive—and deliver them when they are together. "Not bad" and "Okay" are not acceptable praise.
3. The wife will take responsibility to "dress the set" (bedroom). She should plan an evening of intimacy. Her actions might include personal pampering, new sheets, candles, bubbly beverage, wearing the new intimate apparel, music, meeting her husband at the door, etc.

4. After a successful evening at home, the husband needs to plan and execute an intimate surprise overnight get away. He should pack for both (perhaps involving the assistance of her closest friend to ensure he remembers everything important to her) and arrange for childcare if needed.
5. Both partners need to develop a "language of intimacy" that will allow them to address sexual needs and desires comfortably. This builds on the basic skills outlined in The Couple's Communication Exercise found in appendix C. However, while the communication exercise focuses on communicating emotional needs, the "language of intimacy" is directed more toward physical needs. To initiate the use of the "language of intimacy" and become more comfortable talking about physical needs and desires, the couple may start with a back rub that over a period of time evolves into a full body massage, including intimate areas, alternating spouses as the recipient.

Two

Weepy Most of the Time

Depression

The Issue

Sarah is a wife, a mother of two, and a Christian. She and her husband, Stewart, have a happy marriage; she has a fulfilling job, is active in ministry, and spends quality time with her family. Looking at her life, everything appears to be in order. However, for the last year, Sarah has discovered that her energy is low, she has trouble concentrating at work, and she feels weepy most of the time.

Sarah's paternal grandfather was depressed (according to family members) but was undiagnosed medically. Her sister, who is not a Christian, has been medicated for depression for several years and is doing well. Sarah's physician checked her for low thyroid and other ailments without finding any physical cause for her symptoms. He believes that she is depressed and would like to start her on antidepressants.

At the encouragement of well-meaning friends, Sarah has searched her heart for unresolved sin issues. The women in her small group have advised her to put her joy in the Lord, increase her daily prayer time, and wait it out. Stewart thinks this is a spiritual issue and that if she was really a good Christian she would be able to "just snap out of it." Over time, Sarah's depression has turned into a major stress in their marriage. She feels she has tried everything and is in need of help.

The Insights

As the symptoms described in Sarah's situation have gained awareness in the medical community as depression, it has created a conflict within the Christian community. Is this a spiritual issue? Is it a medical issue? Where do we draw the lines? While there is no way this brief chapter will resolve this controversy, we do hope to shed some light on the subject by sharing what others have done in similar situations and to offer the advice—though sometimes conflicting—of professionals. The difference of opinion represented here reflects the ongoing debate.

If you or your spouse struggle with depression, we encourage you to prayerfully read through the following pages to help determine which course of action is best for you. Solutions for depression tend to fall into two camps. We are calling one "nourish your soul" and the other "take your pills." Both have proven to be effective for different people.

We believe that anytime a condition, such as depression, is threatening the foundation of an otherwise solid marriage, loving extravagantly may mean setting aside your own beliefs on the issue and doing what it takes to help your spouse.

Depression

Some people believe that depression is always a spiritual issue and should be handled with a strictly spiritual cure. While there may be sin issues that need to be addressed, and dealing with them may help, simply telling someone to "get right with the Lord" usually does more harm than good.

In talking about her own depression, one of our peer advisors, Barb, said,

> I didn't want the ladies in my Bible study to know. I was scared they would think I was a sham.

Another peer, Robin, agrees:

> I have been in Sarah's shoes and found the Christian community, even pastors, eager to "shoot the wounded" with arrows of false guilt, ignorance, and fear. One of the most urgent needs in the church today is simple, solid teaching that depression is a real medical illness and that medicine and psychotherapy are legitimate tools that God can use.

Chuck worked with a seventeen-year-old girl who was depressed. She had been to four different pastors who told her that it was all in her head and that she needed to get right with God. The guilt and hopelessness created by their well-meaning counsel resulted in an attempted suicide. As Chuck worked with her, it was discovered that she had adult ADHD and was put on medication. She went from being suicidal to graduating from college, getting married, and going on to lead a normal life.

Nourish Your Soul

If a person like Sarah has searched his or her life for potential "sin issues" or other causes and not found any unresolved concerns—yet the depression remains—there are still many non-medical options available. I call these "nourishing your soul," and all of us need an element of them in our lives—whether or not we are facing depression.

As Barb did, you might want to try these before going the medical route or in conjunction with it. After reading Sarah's story, Barb wrote:

> I have been there. On the outside I was the motivator and the upbeat person in every group in which I was involved. When I came home, I started falling apart. I often felt like crying and only got out of bed because I knew my children needed me. My kindergartner was always late to school because I couldn't find the keys to drive the car. My doctor suggested I might be experiencing depression.

A Spiritual Battle. Chuck adds, "Depression is one of the enemy's best tools to distance people from God. He loves it when people do not get help."

Sylvia is a nurse, a wife of thirty-nine years, and a mother of six children. She has battled depression for twenty years. From her personal and professional experience, she adds,

> Depression is often a battle of the mind that Satan uses to condemn us and to plant worrisome, anxious, and negative thoughts. We must equip ourselves and renew our mind as Ephesians 4:22–24 instructs; we cannot wallow in negative thoughts. Police your thoughts and when negative ones begin, fill your mind with the Word of God (Eph. 6:13, 17). Meditate on verses like Joshua 1:9, "I command you—be strong and courageous! Do not be afraid or discouraged. For the LORD your God is with you wherever you go" (NLT). As a depressed person, it is sometimes hard to get the fuzz out of your mind to concentrate. Sometimes taking a simple verse such as Psalm 23:1 and saying it over and over like this helps:
>
> > The LORD is my shepherd.
> > The LORD *is* my shepherd.
> > The LORD is *my* shepherd.
> > The LORD is my *shepherd.*
>
> Remember the instruction in Philippians 4:8 to fill your mind with everything that is beautiful. There is a battleground in the mind, and we must become good warriors and learn to fight. Don't let negative, depressing thoughts consume you.

Take Care of Your Body. Sylvia encourages Sarah by saying that she is doing many things right. Since we are created in spirit, mind, and body, we need to take care of all three. Sylvia admonishes Sarah to look at all the options. She says,

> The medical community wants to throw medicine at anyone

with depression, but there are other ways. Some studies show that depressed people usually have low serotonin or dopamine levels. Exercise increases the levels of these good chemicals. I recommend adding something in your life in the way of exercise, like water aerobics, tennis, golf, walking the dog, swimming. Put something creative in your life; take watercolor classes, decorate birdhouses, plant a garden. The act of creating causes good things to happen. Filling your mind with the beautiful and powerful words of God's love in Scripture is good—or reading a lovely devotional book. Laughter is helpful. Singing increases good chemicals—even in the shower. But stress increases bad ones.

Like Sarah, Chuck has a family history of depression, and he has battled it most of his life. He has found that exercise makes a major difference in his life. He likes to mountain bike. I prefer to rollerblade. When I am out of town he usually rides his bike, and when I am in town we make a major effort to rollerblade together, often spending three hours at a stretch in physical activity—even in the dead of winter! While I do not have a constant struggle with the "black dog," as Winston Churchill called depression, I find that exercise is important for me too. It is one of the ways I "nourish my soul."

Barb's doctor recommended that she get some exercise daily, take a walk. He also advised her to cut back on any non-required responsibilities and find a hobby or interest she could get passionate about. As a result, today, Barb reports,

> It's working! I walk, garden (the fresh air certainly helps), and paint. My husband noticed I am smiling more and playing with the kids and him more. I think many women tend to overextend themselves and not even realize it—whether they are working or stay-at-home moms. Stay-at-home moms feel they need to prove they did something all day and working moms feel they need to make up for the time they spend at work. The result is we are all stressed out. God doesn't expect us to do it all, and He doesn't need us to do it all! He just wants us to love

and worship Him. Once I cleared away the unnecessary noise in my life, I could enjoy God's gifts.

Chuck and I have also found that his eating habits drastically affect his moods. If he eats well and regularly, his mood is more stable. If I sense he is getting irritable and grumpy, I'll ask, "When was the last time you ate?" He has learned this coded communication and asks, "Am I grumpy?" For my own sanity, I try to keep some protein with me when we travel, and he has learned to take responsibility for eating what he has learned his body needs. Even while I am at home writing, I often have dinner in the crock-pot waiting for him the moment he walks in the door. This is one way I can love him extravagantly.

Sylvia agrees and advises Sarah to check her nutrition.

> Is she skipping breakfast or lunch? Is she low on iron, vitamins A or K, calcium, or magnesium? Depression can be caused by poor nutrition.

Take a Look at Your Life. Sylvia encourages Sarah to look at her life.

> Do you need a different kind of life? A new job? Are you overwhelmed with work and family? Do you have relationships that are upsetting you? Do you feel loved and valued? Do you have a heart friend—one to whom you can tell it like it is?

Sometimes making changes in the things that we can change can make a big difference. It may take some time to implement changes, but if you do not start now, nothing will change. Maybe you need to begin taking some classes to enhance your skills for a new career. In my book, *The Praying Wives Club* (coauthored with my friend Dianne), we offer extensive guidance for developing a group of "heart friends" with whom you pray regularly—specifically for your marriage.

Consider Herbal Alternatives. Other times, we can clearly see the stressors that are causing the depression, yet are unable to do anything about it. A few years ago, economic forces caused Chuck to live in Colorado for five months while I had to stay in New Mexico. They were very difficult months—as were the months immediately before and after. During that time, I cried at the drop of a hat. I felt like I was on the verge of tears all the time. I cried out to God, and I often cried myself to sleep, alone in our big bed—except for my fluffy schnauzer who I made sleep next to me even though he prefers the floor. I knew the exact cause of my depression, and I could see that Chuck and I were making the best of a very difficult situation. But, that did not mean that I liked it! I started taking St. John's Wort and found that it helped stabilize my moods and helped get me through that difficult time.

Sylvia suggests that if Sarah has tried these "nourish your soul" approaches and they have not made a noticeable positive change, that she should then look at taking something natural, like St. John's Wort or SAMe (S-Adenosyl-Methionine). These "natural" remedies are controversial, but many people have found them helpful. If you struggle with depression, you might want to do some additional research on the herbal alternatives. Many traditional doctors are now familiar with the "natural" remedies and are excellent sources of information. In addition, herbs are still a form of medicine and can have serious side effects. I would recommend consulting a doctor before taking any herbal remedy.

Take Your Pills

Clinical Depression—More Than a Spiritual Issue. Sarah's doctor wants to put her on antidepressants. Sarah's sister has been taking them successfully for several years. Sarah's grandfather also struggled with depression, though in his time depression was not labeled as a medical condition. These factors combine to indicate that Sarah's condition—which contains all the symptoms of classic depression—is more than a spiritual issue. Gaylen Larson, PhD, says of Sarah's case,

> She may have a biochemical imbalance as well as a heredity precondition. We know that depression runs in families, just like diabetes. If you are trying to deal with the symptom instead of the cause, you will never have true victory.

If the depression is truly a chemical imbalance and a hereditary issue, some form of medication may be needed. It should be looked at not as something that will cure the problem, but rather to keep it in check—just like insulin is for a diabetic. Neither Sarah nor her husband should expect that medication for her depression will be something that she takes for a few months and then gets over the depression. Antidepressants are not addictive. Studies of long-term use (10 years) show no adverse affects.

There does seem to be a long-term benefit of the medication. The brain appears to "rewire" itself even after the medication is discontinued. Like any medicine, antidepressants must be used with the careful supervision of an experienced psychiatrist. Women should see a psychiatrist who understands menopausal/hormonal fluctuations and their impact on depression.

If you are in a similar situation to Sarah's and your doctor has checked hormones and chemical balances like thyroid function, and they are all okay, listen to your doctor and take the recommended medications. If your husband hesitates, have the doctor or some other trusted individual like your pastor (if he is in agreement) talk frankly with your husband. You may need to get medical attention before you hit bottom, are hospitalized, and have the stigma of mental illness added to your concerns. Depression can be hereditary, but siblings may not show symptoms at the same age. Spiritual and marital problems are often the result of depression due to the response of others and their attitude toward this kind of chemical imbalance.

The longer depression goes without treatment, the harder it is to reverse—even to the point that it becomes irreversible.

Short-Term Help. A pastor's wife I met at a conference told me that her husband had been opposed to medication for depression until she had a bout with it that virtually incapacitated her. She was placed on medication for long enough to lift her out of the darkness. She did not have the family history or the other symptoms that would indicate a long need for medication.

Chuck says that for some people a depression comes upon them due to circumstances, medical reasons, or a combination of both. Once they are in the pit of depression, life looks so bleak that they cannot see their way through to the light at the end of the tunnel. In these cases, medication is helpful to lift them up enough that they can deal with their situation in a logical and rational manner. Once the situation has been addressed and dealt with, the medication is no longer needed. Such was the case with this pastor's wife. Her husband is now a believer that sometimes medication is the best option.

Ann told us the following story:

> When I was forty-two, I was so depressed that I was considering bloodless ways to commit suicide. (I didn't want to leave any ugly stains.) Finally I sought help. I started interviewing counselors, and it took each of them about thirty-two seconds to diagnose me as clinically depressed—even though logically I could tell myself that my life was great. The medication prescribed by my psychiatrist began to remove the bleakness in about twenty to thirty days. It took nine months before I did not need it anymore. Through the combination of medication and counseling, I learned to change my destructive behavior patterns.
>
> Eight years later, I am happier than I have ever been in my life—even though my husband's company was downsized and he took early retirement, we're facing an empty nest, my mom's health is declining, and I'm starting a new career as primary breadwinner (all significant life changes). No matter how much I prayed, I doubt I would have had the insights I gained through counseling. Just being faithful does not insulate us from depression, illness, poor judgment, or misfortune.

As Bev said about her friend,

> How wonderful that today we know she has a chemical problem. Women like Sarah should not fiddle around with this. It actually can be life threatening if it escalates into certain types of problems. From what we see in the case history, Sarah has evidence of depression, but she does not know what chemical

imbalance is feeding it nor what may develop from this point. Catching it close to the beginning of the slide is more effective than waiting to see if it becomes a full-blown illness. Yes, God can heal her. If He does, the medications will not hurt her, and her response can be seen as evidence of less or no need for them. In the meantime, take action.

Depression Is Real

Depression is a real issue. While both Chuck and I have had periods of depression with different probable causes and different approaches to treatment, I was surprised at the volume of response and the degree of passion I received when I posted Sarah's scenario. Depression is a real problem for many people today, even strong believers in healthy Christian marriages.

If depression is a factor in your marriage, do not let it ruin your relationship. You might try the non-medical solutions first—after all, exercise and activities that stimulate us are good for everyone, depressed or not. If the medical answer turns out to be the right one for you, the non-medical activities can only increase the medication's effectiveness. However, Mike Sievert, MD, advises,

> Do not mix the herbal remedies with the conventional antidepressants, and be sure to be under supervision of a psychiatrist who is familiar with the treatment of depression and its possible side effects.

Whichever approach works for you, follow the advice of our peers and professionals and take your depression seriously.

The Interactions

For couples in a similar situation to Sarah and Stewart, Chuck would assign the following "homework" assignment:

1. Both parties need to agree to mutually submit as delineated in Ephesians.
2. The spouse with concerns about treatment should take the initiative to learn about depression. He or she might achieve this by going to the local medical library—perhaps at a university—or searching the Internet with the goal of finding documented, scientific research on both sides of the depression debate. ("Documented, scientific" is suggested because the Internet is full of odd sites.)
3. The couple should then meet together with a Christian psychiatrist. They should go prepared with questions addressing their educated concerns and objections.
4. The spouse with depressed tendencies needs to continue pursuing all avenues of spiritual and natural (diet and exercise) solutions.
5. Also, visit the family doctor to rule out any other medical causes such as menopausal/hormonal fluctuations or thyroid dysfunction.
6. As all of the solutions proposed within the chapter are good options, the couple should commit to pursuing all options without bias. Many people feel torn within the power struggle of which model is better which only exacerbates the issue.

Three

Childless by Choice

Outside Pressures, a Full and Happy Life

The Issue

"Yes, I will marry you, but there will be no children." Dena can still remember saying those words more than twenty years ago. Her husband-to-be, Brad, was more than willing to agree to the "no children" clause. Both had been extremely hurt in their first marriages and had built major walls to protect themselves from any further pain.

The years have rolled on. They have a good marriage, not a great one, but still better than some. They love each other. Seven years into the marriage, Dena reached thirty. She began asking herself the very difficult question: "Do I want to remain childless for the rest of my life?" On one hand, they had become very selfish with their time and money and having a baby would really upset the apple cart. On the other hand, they were the only couple in both families to remain childless. Dena was not pressuring herself, but was feeling pressure from family members, friends, people with whom she worked, even members of their church. She has been amazed how cruel some people can be simply because you do not meet their expectations of how you should live your life.

While Brad and Dena are happy with their place in life and their decision, the pressure put on them by other well-meaning people has made Dena question her life. She is having trouble sleeping, roaming the house at night with her mind playing the same old tune over and over again: "You are such a disappointment to everyone."

Both Brad and Dena have good jobs that they enjoy. However, after twenty years of marriage they feel they are missing something.

The Insights

While at first glance, it may seem that this situation applies to very few, the responses we received indicate that it is indeed an issue in need of some fresh insights. Laura wrote,

> I know making a choice to not have children isn't a popular option, and I certainly don't expect many others to share it. Occasionally I run across a woman who is brave enough to express the same emotions. We connect instantly because most people think we are weird. I am responding because I've rarely seen anyone brave enough to address this topic.

Laura's words ring true for many couples, including us. Whether "brave" or foolish, if you are willing to say, "I made this choice and I am okay with it," the response is emphatic. Most every childless couple has felt, at some time or another, shunned or misplaced by their status.

In discussing her childless status, Melody says,

> I have felt like an outsider in society. I used to dread meeting new people who would invariably ask if we had children. In shaking my head, I felt like I was confessing to a crime or admitting I had a terrible deformity.

Some of those who offered their stories are like Laura, Dena, and me. We either knew all along that we did not want children, or, biology ticked by and we never had any. Others, like Melody and her husband, Pride, and JoAnn and her husband, Brian, wanted children only to find that they were unable to conceive. JoAnn reported,

We have experienced society's condemning looks when we have told them we do not have children, especially when we have not explained why. We stopped explaining because it was actually easier to receive "the look" that condemned us as selfish than it was to explain everything we had gone through and have people say, "Don't worry, it will happen."

When Amanda and Tony got married, they decided not to have children. Then after a few years of marriage they decided they did want children, but "try as we might, it didn't happen." Of the pressure of meeting others' expectations, she says,

> No one has given me a hard time about not having children because I have found it easier to say, "We tried and it didn't work." I have a sense that if I hadn't used that line; people would have pushed harder.

In a magazine article titled, "Married Without Children: A Curse or a Call?" Jan Coleman writes,

> A couple in their early forties was constantly asked, "What if everybody decided not to have children?" The wife stated, "It bewilders most people and makes them uneasy. Somehow, they think we selfishly opted for fun and freedom over the love of a child. Rarely does anyone understand."[1]

Whew! It is not just me who has felt the pressure. I remember visiting with a noted Christian author. When the conversation came to the inevitable subject of children and he found out that I did not have any, he vowed to pray for me stating, "Everyone I pray for gets pregnant!" "Don't you dare," I ventured. Yes, my mother is disappointed that there are no "little Maritas." She finally quit asking about children when I quipped, "I will have them when you stay home and take care of them." Or perhaps it was around the time that Chuck and I had been married for eighteen years without children that she gave up.

The pressure Dena feels is real. First we'll look at dealing with the pressures and expectations of others and then living a full and happy life without children. Whether your situation matches Brad and Dena's—or like Melody, JoAnn, and Amanda you wanted children but never had them—you will find help on the following pages.

Outside Pressures

Determine God's Leading

While our case history does not give us the details of why Dena and Brad made the decision not to have children, we do know that it is a decision they agreed upon and we can assume, as Melody mentions, they feel secure in that choice.

Melody and Pride had postponed having children to deal with their own issues. Melody says,

> For the first twelve years of our marriage, my husband and I were engrossed with completing our education and establishing our careers. We had many hurdles to cross before children could be considered. Like Dena, I brought many scars into my marriage, so I sought counseling in order to work through some of my "baggage." After really working through those issues and finally feeling ready to start a family, I found out I had fertility problems. After trying all kinds of medical intervention, we finally decided to give up. Although many people encouraged us to adopt, we felt we just were not ready for that. Many people looked down on us for not adopting immediately, as if our desire for a child wasn't sincere. However, we felt that we were being obedient to God's leading.

Like Melody and Pride, JoAnn and Brian feel that God has led them to the place of being a childless couple. JoAnne says,

> After over seven years of infertility treatments—and failures—Brian and I also are seriously considering the *choice* of remaining childless. We believe that if it was God's will that we have

children, one of the treatments would have worked. We have also concluded that if we do not have children He must have a path and purpose for our lives that could not be accomplished if we did have children. We find that prospect very exciting. We could still make the choice to defy His will and continue alternative ways to have a child and could even be successful. We believe that if we pursued that path we would not be living God's "best" life for us. Although we would not wish the pain of infertility on anyone, we have watched our faith grow in ways we know it would not have otherwise.

Free Yourself from Others' Expectations

When we as a couple operate outside of what the rest of the world considers the norm, we will always be asked questions, or at least given "the look," as JoAnn described. Melody addresses others' expectations.

> Like any lifestyle choice—especially one outside of the standard routine—not everyone will understand. For instance, several missionary friends of mine tell me their families reject the choice they have made to serve the Lord in a foreign country for little pay. They must constantly protect the choice they have made from criticism by others. However, they are able to do this because they have a firm commitment to their choice, they have a sense of inner peace about it, and they believe it is their appointed path from God. Remaining childless is a very valid choice that can be freeing and rewarding in many ways. However, because it is not the usual choice people make, couples need to feel very secure about their decision, or they will needlessly feel isolated and inferior.

Addressing others' expectations in the decision to have children or not, Chuck says, "All of us must strive to guide our lives with our own internal compass. It is always a mistake to live out the expectations or unfulfilled wishes of others—especially our parents. The role to produce grandchildren is perhaps the most common and powerful instance of inheriting a debt. If an individual can learn to deal with this issue successfully, all the others will be easy! To be free of the expectations of others and to live within God's will is free indeed."

While I never set out not to have children, I do believe, as do Melody and JoAnn, that remaining childless is the path God has for my life. There are many things that God has uniquely equipped me for and that I have accomplished that I could not have done if I had children. I did not have a burning desire to have children, although when I got married I assumed that I would, because that is what one did.

When Chuck and I got married, we agreed to wait three years before doing anything permanent to prevent pregnancy. Three years came and we still did not feel ready to make a decision either way. We agreed to wait five years, then ten. I trust that if God wanted me to be a mother, He would have placed that desire in me so strongly that I could not ignore it. My sister, raised the same as I was, knew from childhood that she wanted to be a mom. I was a tomboy. I played with cars, not dolls. I was entrepreneurial from the time I was four years old. Today, my sister has children and puppies. I have a business and cars.

Stand by Your Decision

Having the confidence that you have made the right choice for your life is a key to dealing with the projections and expectations others put upon you. Roseanne Elling, LPC, advises,

> If the husband and the wife are both secure in the Lord about this decision, He is the foundation and peace that they can fall back on when confronted by hurtful people. Communicate the certainty of the choice to not have children with confident nonverbal cues such as looking the other person in the eye and speaking with a relaxed and confident tone of voice. Knowing you are doing God's will for your life is a huge confidence booster. People tend to accept what we say more readily if we believe it! If the husband and wife can both say "we" instead of "I" when responding, each partner will feel additional support—even in the absence of the other—and the hearer

of their response will likely respect the strength of a united decision.

When a couple is confident that they've selected what's best for them—childless by choice or by acceptance—they can more easily deal with the pressures the world, the church, and the family put on them to fit into the norm. Laura says,

> My not having children has been by choice, but it's not that way for every woman. I am satisfied with that decision, and now that I am forty-five I don't look back and regret it.

Genetics Are a Consideration

In addition to my lack of maternal instincts and the true belief that I am walking the path God has set before me, I have other reasons for not pushing to have children. Many people have heard my mother's testimony and know that she lost two boys to brain damage. But few connect that story to me. Those boys were my younger brothers. Most people are unaware of the rest of our history. My grandmother, my mother's mother, lost a child in infancy. I remember talking about this with my grandmother's sister, "Aunt Jean." She was disappointed that I would choose not to have children. When I brought up the family history with her, she indignantly replied, "There was nothing the matter with Arthur."

However, seventy-five years ago when Arthur was born, diagnostic tests were not available as they are today. There were not always labels for diseases or illnesses. He just died. So Aunt Jean clung to the belief that there was nothing wrong with her sister's baby. We do not know. There may not have been, but there may have been some problem as well. We do know that he died in infancy.

In my generation, my sister lost a child mid-term with Down's syndrome. So, I have a family history of three generations of problem births. My sister has three beautiful, healthy boys. If I had felt the desire as strongly as she did to have children, I am sure that I would have—even with the history. But history confirmed my choice for me. As was stated by the wife in Jan Coleman's article, "Rarely does anyone understand."

There Are Benefits

I encourage Dena and Brad to look at their choice and why they made it. When Amanda and her husband decided not to have children, they interviewed elderly couples who didn't have children. Amanda reports,

> They are the ones who held hands and said "honey" a lot! They seemed to still be dating at seventy!

Victoria Jackson, LCSW, adds,

> It is more healthy to enjoy a rich couple relationship than to have children simply because it is "expected" and be resentful of the time and energy children take. Once you are a parent, you are in it for life!

A Full and Happy Life

Those whose lives revolve around their children look at those of us without children and know that we are missing out. Yes, we are missing out on the joys of parenting that they experience, but we can still have a full and happy life with different experiences. In Jan Coleman's article, she quotes a couple, Linda and Craig, who say,

> Not everybody was meant to have children in their life. As with the whole Christian life, when you accept your situation, you can find many joys and options in it.

What "Makes" a Marriage?

Having children is not what makes a marriage. In their book *Living with Infertility,* Roger and Robin Sonnenberg write,

> In words that many infertile (and childless) couples will find affirming, the late Christian counselor Walter Trobisch

addressed childless marriages. He quoted Genesis 2:24, "Therefore, a man leaves his father and his mother and cleaves to his wife and they become one flesh." Trobisch then asked how this verse ends, and a man replied, "With a full stop," or period. Trobisch emphasized this "full stop," noting that in that key verse about marriage, a verse quoted four times in the Bible, there is not a word about children. "The effect of these words on my audience was tremendous," he recalled. "It was as if I had thrown a bomb into the church."

"Don't misunderstand me," he continued. "Children are a blessing of God." The Bible emphasizes this over and over again . . . children are a blessing to marriage, but they are an additional blessing to marriage. When God created Adam and Eve, he blessed them and then said to them: "Be fruitful and multiply." From the Hebrew text it is clear that this commandment was an additional action to the action of blessing. Therefore, when the Bible describes the indispensable elements of marriage, it is significant that children are not expressly mentioned. Leaving, cleaving, and becoming one flesh are sufficient. The full stop means that the child does not make marriage a marriage. A childless marriage is also a marriage in the full sense of the word.[2]

Connect with Other Children

Not only are those of us couples without children in a "full marriage," but also as non-parent adults we can often have a positive influence on children and youth that their own parents cannot have.

Sharing her experience, Amanda writes,

> I've found that through the years, I have had a profound influence on friends' children. When they wouldn't speak to their parents, they would speak to me because I was cool and not a parent. Even now, I have a sixteen-year-old girl who frequently comes over to our house, just to talk to me. Imagine, a sixteen-year-old girl wanting advice from a fifty-three-year-old woman!

Another peer, Leigh, responded because she and her husband related to Dena and Brad's situation. They too had faced pressure from parents and began to question their choice. In 1995, Leigh had the opportunity to go on a work camp with the teenagers from their church. She reports:

> Work camp was a wonderful experience and I felt led to continue working with teenagers. Although I have to admit that it seemed a bit odd that the Lord would direct my steps to work with these young people when I had never even had a baby. I asked the Lord one day, "Why me?" His answer was that because I never wanted babies, He would give me the biggest babies of all, namely teenagers. I have worked with these young people for over five years now and taken six road trips with them, and yes, they are my babies. I love working with these kids for they give a dimension to my life that I had never known before.

She asked them why they worked together so well and was told that it was because she had never been someone's mom, just someone's kid.

> They see me as a non-threatening adult—just a much older teenager. We don't have children of our own to call us Mom and Dad, and we will never have grandchildren to call us Grandma and Grandpa, but we have spiritual children galore. We are very blessed indeed!

I feel like Leigh when she says that she has many spiritual children. Sometimes when I am asked if I have children, I say, "Yes, hundreds." I feel very maternal toward the speakers and authors I help train through the CLASSeminar. I feel like a proud mother hen each time I receive a book in the mail that has been published as a result of my involvement in the author's life. These speakers and authors are my children, even though some of them are actually older than I am and have children my age.

I remember with great fondness the influence of Aunt Jean in my life. She died at ninety years old while I was in the midst of writing a book. I did not hesitate for a moment to drop everything and cross the country to attend her memorial service. Many of us had tears in our eyes as we shared "Aunt Jean" stories. With her as my role model, I have tried to be that kind of person for my nephews. They come and visit us for a week at a time, much as I did with Aunt Jean when I was child. Chuck and I have taken our nephews motorcycle riding, shooting, and hiking—things they do not do at home.

Chuck and I have done similar things for his nieces. His sister has been a single parent for much of her daughters' lives and their father has not been consistently involved. When Chuck's elder niece got married, she asked him to walk her down the aisle—which he was honored to do. When his younger niece was in a tough place, she came to live with us for several months.

Melody shares that she and her husband both remember some person in their lives who was not a parent but who had an enormous amount of influence on their lives. She says,

> My husband and I feel that God has asked us to do this kind of service for kids who are already here, rather than to produce children of our own. Not everyone will understand this, and certainly not everyone is called to it. However, we feel strongly that we would not have the energy, time, or ability to do these things if we had a family of our own. Though we didn't originally think so, we are now sure that God put this path in front of us and that it is His perfect will for us. Most of the children with whom we work come from poor homes and have emotional or academic problems that severely hinder them. We don't think it is an easy task to work with them to try to help them improve—but it is a task that brings us great joy!

Chuck reminds Dena and Brad, and all childless couples, that there are so many children and teens in need of adults who are willing to make an investment in them. Many technically "childless" teachers, counselors, social workers, youth ministers, and extended family members are making a greater contribution to the next generation than some parents. It is not the genetic material contributed that counts, it's the sum contribution to the welfare and Christian upbringing of the children that matters.

Perhaps you can benefit by the advice for Dena and Brad; search your heart before God and ask Him what is His path for your life. As you can tell from the sampling of stories shared here, it may be His plan that you not have children. But don't hold back on the extravagant love He has placed within you. Great joy is out there for you. The maternal instinct doesn't stop at your own doorstep.

The Interactions

Whether you are in a similar situation to Dena and Brad or are facing the expectations of others on an issue other than childlessness, Chuck would assign the following "homework" assignment:

1. Write out a list of expectations others have of you, including who expressed (or implied) them.
2. Evaluate each expectation and who it came from for validity. Challenge each expectation asking yourself, "Does this person have a right to set expectations for my life?" "Am I honoring this person's expectations out of my desires or out of guilt?"
3. Write out your expectations of each other as husband and wife. As a couple, these expectations are to be taken very seriously. Discuss them as a couple to be sure individual assumptions are accurate.
4. Write out your expectations of yourself. Each expectation of yourself has to be tested for validity to determine that it is truly your own rather than an expectation someone else has for you.
5. Write out your heart's desire and any call(s) felt; what are God's expectations for your life?
6. Fill in the blank: "My life is missing _____." Make plans to meet that missing need.
7. Review what God has called you to do and your expectations of each other. These are to be your priority. Everyone else's expectations (if valid) are secondary.

Four

Growing Apart

Different Levels of Maturity, Respect and Honor

The Issue

Ed and Elizabeth have been married for fourteen years. They married when they were both brand-new Christians. Ed was barely divorced from his first wife at the time. They married more from their mutual dysfunctions and neediness rather than from a whole heart desiring to give and to love one another. After all these years, both of them have been through many changes. Elizabeth, a Popular Sanguine/Powerful Choleric, has spent a great deal of time with God, counselors, and self-help books and sees herself as an entirely different person. She feels she can now relate to and experience a much healthier relationship. However from Elizabeth's point of view, Ed, a Perfect Melancholy, has not grown as she has. She believes she has overcome so many things only to find that her husband has not come with her, nor does he want to. Ed and Elizabeth are currently seeing a counselor and considering divorce.

The Insights

Given what we know about Elizabeth and Ed, two key factors can make an almost instant difference in this troubled relationship that may be applicable in your relationship as well: first, maturity, and then respect and honor. Since we have limited facts in this case, we have addressed the subject with a broad brush in hopes of touching not only Ed and Elizabeth's situation, but circumstances in your life as well. As I speak to women's groups across the country, I find many marriages where one spouse is more spiritually or emotionally mature than the other.

Different Levels of Maturity

Since Elizabeth says that she has grown both as a person and a Christian, let's accept that she is more mature than Ed. Chuck advises, however, that if she has grown out of her marriage, maybe she hasn't really grown at all. As a Christian, Elizabeth needs to look at the overall teaching of God's Word. Throughout the Bible she will find many verses that point to God's belief in marriage and its priority. For example, Matthew 19:4–6 says,

> "Haven't you read," [Jesus] replied, "that at the beginning the Creator 'made them male and female,' and said, 'For this reason a man will leave his father and mother and be united to his wife, and the two will become one flesh'? So they are no longer two, but one. Therefore what God has joined together, let man not separate." (NIV)

Remember, God never advises us to do something that is contrary to the overall teachings in His Word. If your growth has caused you to be unhappy with your spouse, is that what God wants?

Elizabeth's story hit home for Lindsay as she, too, seeks growth at a different pace than her husband. This was her second marriage and it, like Elizabeth and Ed's, was near divorce. From her experience as a peer, Lindsay suggests that Elizabeth look at what she has learned from all those self-help books.

> Is there anything you have learned that is contrary to the Word of God? Does God want to tear up marriages or strengthen

them? What lies are you listening to, nourishing, or heeding that you would consider divorce?

Additionally, Chuck often advises people to throw away their self-help books that focus on "self." The biblical mandate is not to watch out for self, but to display Christ-like love—extravagant love—toward others. He suggests that if a book, or an activity, doesn't draw us closer to God and closer to our spouse, it is doing more harm than good. Use that as the yardstick to measure marital satisfaction.

I am a great fan of Gary Thomas's work, especially his book *Sacred Marriage*. I suggest that Elizabeth read it carefully. In it, Gary says,

> It is not the better part of godliness to let one's spiritual duties eclipse one's marital responsibilities. What most divorces mean is that at least one party, and possibly both, have ceased to put the gospel first in their lives. They no longer live by Paul's guiding principle, "I make it my goal to please Him," because the Bible makes it clear in its teaching. God says, "I hate divorce." (Mal. 2:16) If the goal of the couple was to please God, they wouldn't seek divorce.[1]

Melanie Wilson adds,

> Christian women often pursue a spiritual journey without including their husbands. I always recommend that couples communicate what they're learning and why they're excited, without the expectation that the spouse will follow the same path. We can easily use our growth as a way of one-upping our spouse. When I became very excited about daily prayer and Bible study through Becky Tirabassi's materials, I could tell that my husband felt left out. I bought him his own Bible and prayer journal and he feels more included—even though he does not use them the way I do.

Grow Together

Gaylen Larson, PhD, encourages Elizabeth to include her husband in her growth process as Melanie has included hers.

It's important for Elizabeth to look at how she might be pushing Ed away by her self-help growth. He will not want to discuss subjects that make him feel "less-than." If she can structure the discussion about a book as asking for his advice or hold the discussion in such a way that his opinion is held in high regard, it will no longer be a threat. She may find him unconsciously wanting to be more involved.

With Maturity Comes Responsibility

To help her reframe her situation, Lindsay—figuratively speaking—wrote on the tablet of her heart. She encourages anyone in Elizabeth's place to do the same thing.

> One hundred times a day "write," *Divorce is not an option. Divorce is not an option....* Or, make it more of a positive affirmation: *By my submitting to God, our marriage is a source of comfort and joy* or *In marriage, my husband and I not only survive, but thrive.*

First, one must accept the concept that divorce is not an option. Next, if the woman is the more spiritually mature—which is often true—she holds the responsibility to love her husband unconditionally with the Lord's love. (Of course, if the man was the more mature, he would hold that responsibility.) Again we look to God's Word for guidance. Repeatedly the Bible admonishes us to love one another as Christ loved us—especially the unlovable. In a difficult marriage, the unlovable is often the spouse. If one spouse claims to be the stronger Christian, she/he holds the greater responsibility to display that love.

In our case history couple, Elizabeth needs to love her husband, as he is, not expecting anything in return—not to get, but to give. When she does this, she will find that her husband is apt to be more responsive to growth himself.

Respect and Honor

This brings us to the idea of respect and honor. Another peer advisor, Sylvia, offers this insight,

> My husband of thirty-nine years is also a Perfect Melancholy. Like Elizabeth, I am Popular Sanguine/Powerful Choleric. Through the years, I have learned several things. I've learned that my husband thrives on admiration and respect. If he senses he is not meeting my expectations, he withdraws. My expectations make him feel judged and cause an atmosphere that is not loving, creating a worsening cycle. Jesus tells me that my job is loving, not judging.

In their book *Intimate Allies,* Dan Allender and Tremper Longman III spotlight this concept.

> Marriage requires a radical commitment to love our spouses as they are, while longing for them to be what they are not yet. Every marriage moves either toward enhancing one another's glory or toward degrading each other.[2]

Pray for a Mentor

Lindsay encourages women in a similar situation to Elizabeth to pray for a "spiritual mother," a mature older woman with a solid marriage to whom she can go for help. Lindsay says,

> Once when I was irritated at my husband, I asked my spiritual mother what she did when she wanted to "pop her husband in the chops." She laughed and told me to pray and ask God to give me His love for my husband when I don't have any love of my own.

Lindsay knows from experience that God is faithful to answer this prayer!

Encourage, Don't Try to Change

Another aspect of this situation is the couple's personalities. Again, Elizabeth needs to take the lead. By nature, the Popular Sanguine is the most inclined to change. The Popular Sanguine wants everyone to be happy. She can make adjustments in herself if it will make the other person happy. I claim Romans 12:18 here: "If it is possible, as far as it depends on you, live at peace with everyone" (NIV). I believe that God added the beginning disclaimer because it is impossible to be at peace with all men. After all, we can only control our own behaviors—but we can control them! The second part of the verse puts the responsibility for peace in the relationship on us, not expecting the other person to change.

Sylvia says,

> My husband is only going to read *Consumer's Report*, the *Wall Street Journal*, and our local newspaper. I am an avid reader and a self-improver. I can make any changes I want in my own behavior, but have only the power to make my own decisions and choices.

Lindsay suggests that women like Elizabeth stop "fiddling" with trying to force changes on their husbands and leave the changing to the Holy Spirit. She says,

> I have this image of my husband and the Holy Spirit on a football field. The Holy Spirit does not need me down on my husband's playing field, but in his grandstand. I hope I have the grace to cheer him on instead of booing him. I think it is deplorable when fans boo the home team!

Chuck agrees with Lindsay's concept. He sees the need for Elizabeth to offer more encouragement and support to Ed, to compliment him frequently. His counsel to Elizabeth is to identify the strengths of the marriage. One strength is that the marriage has provided her with an environment conducive to personal growth. Perhaps she has overlooked that and attributes all of her growth to the self-help books.

Michelle Holman invites encouragement.

> I would also encourage Elizabeth to begin creating a "gratitude list" in a journal. Each day list at least three of Ed's qualities or actions that she observed for which she was grateful. As she begins to embrace an attitude of gratitude toward Ed, I suggest that she share these with him.

Sylvia talks about her own marriage:

> Sometimes we can focus on the negatives rather than the positives. When a negative about him begins to obsess my mind, I find stopping and making a list of all his wonderful attributes helps give me a better perspective. "I" statements spoken in truth and love help release hurt feelings. I try to stay away from the "you" or "if you would only" statements which seem like a put down.

While it is much easier to say than to do, a woman in Elizabeth's situation needs to lovingly submit to her husband, not because he deserves it, but because she is really submitting to the Lord when she honors and respects her husband.

What about you? Whether you are the husband or the wife, are there factors in common with Ed and Elizabeth's marriage and yours? What can you learn from their situation?

The Interactions

For couples in a similar situation to Elizabeth and Ed, Chuck would assign the following "homework" assignment:

For the Wife

1. Describe specifically how things would be different if your husband were the spiritual heavyweight in the home. The greater the detail the better.
2. List what you are doing to bring about your half of the ideal home that you envision.
3. List specifically what you expect from your husband in achieving this goal. How would your husband be different if he were the spiritual leader of the home? Have you given him permission and the opportunity to be the spiritual leader or has he been in a one-down position where he feels that he cannot compete?
4. What role has your spouse played in the current level of growth that you now enjoy?

For the Husband

1. Describe the changes you have seen in your wife over the years and how you feel about them.
2. What steps are you willing to take to fulfill your role as spiritual leader in the home?

PART 2
CAREER ISSUES

Five

Lack of Time Together

Communication, Creative Time Together

The Issue

John has a job that requires him to travel five days a week, three weeks a month. A Powerful Choleric with some Perfect Melancholy, he thrives with his fast-paced, full life. His weekends are short. He usually arrives home on Friday evening. If his flight is late, sometimes it's after midnight when he opens the front door. Completely exhausted after traveling from one city to another, he catches a few extra hours of sleep on Saturday morning. Then, after brunch with his wife, Joan, he heads straight to his home office to file reports from the past week and prepare for the upcoming week. Joan has her second cup of coffee, reads the morning newspaper, and cleans the kitchen—hoping this Saturday will be different and he will finish early. But the routine remains unchanged.

By late afternoon, he has completed his work and sits down with Joan to discuss plans for Saturday night. Their routine has developed into going out to dinner with friends, going to a movie, or renting a movie and staying home. On Sunday, John joins his friends in a round of golf. Then, he has a late lunch with Joan before packing his bag to leave for another week of work and travel.

Joan's job as a schoolteacher keeps her busy each day, but evenings are lonely. She reads, watches television, has dinner at a restaurant with friends, or telephones her parents. The companionship she expected in marriage is absent and she feels abandoned.

When they married, John was traveling two to three days a week. A few months later, he was promoted to regional sales manager and his travel schedule increased; but, rather than travel four weeks out of the month, he would have one week at home. Joan hoped that meant they would have more time to spend together, but instead, during that week, he works in the office from early morning until late evening. Many times after dinner, he will return to the office to work on projects for the upcoming weeks. Except for having dinner together and John sleeping at home that week, there is little difference in their weekly routine.

Joan understands the demands of John's job, but as a Popular Sanguine, she misses him and the fun they had early in their marriage. Before marriage, they had discussed having a family. John now feels they should not have a baby until his schedule is less hectic. He keeps reassuring Joan that things will not always be this way. She is concerned their marriage is suffering from a lack of time together. Each time she brings the subject up, he argues that he is a good provider and spends as much time as possible with her.

The Insights

In our global workplace, many couples have to spend more and more time apart. Like John, one of you may have a job that requires spending large chunks of time on the road. This often happens in military families as well. Other couples are temporarily separated when one spouse has been transferred and the other has not yet found new employment. In other cases, one spouse may have to spend long periods of time away meeting the needs of extended family. Whatever the circumstances creating the separation, the symptoms are often the same. We have chosen to address two key concerns that are important for keeping a long-distance marriage healthy: communication and creative time together.

Communication

After reading about John and Joan's situation, Shirley—one of our peer advisors—wrote,

> I can relate to John and Joan's story. That was my life for forty-two years. During the last five years, it has really intensified; Nate retired from the Air Force and went with industry. He has traveled to China and Russia almost three times a month. Over the years I have had the full range of emotions: feeling neglected, wanting to divorce and find someone who really "cared more about me than his job," creating arguments to try to get my point across, ignoring him, developing my own interests, pretending I didn't care, gaining sympathy from other people for my "sad state of affairs"—and the list goes on.

From her experience, Shirley suggests that others in a similar situation start by beginning to express thanks for what the away or traveling spouse does do. In John and Joan's case, he comes home faithfully, spends Saturday nights with her, and provides for her. Since we know that John is a Powerful Choleric, we understand that he has a need to be appreciated for all the work he does. He believes he is doing what he needs to do as a husband by providing well for Joan. Men see togetherness much differently than women do; their being in the same room—or house—is often sufficient "together time" for men. How can you incorporate these insights into your own situation?

In talking about her marriage, Shirley adds,

> My Powerful Choleric husband, Nate, did not need to spend any time with friends or even spend Saturday night together [with me]. Being in the same room was great "togetherness" for him. Once I realized that being in the same room with him, even though we didn't converse, fulfilled his "togetherness" idea, I could relax with it.

Staying Connected

For couples who spend large quantities of time apart, it is especially easy for their lives to drift in different directions. To maintain a healthy marriage, couples need to remain in contact with each other and be involved in each other's independent activities, much as they would be if they had dinner together every night.

For me, this was a concern when Chuck's employment caused him to live in Colorado while I stayed in New Mexico. As in John and Joan's case, Chuck did not seem as bothered by the situation as I was. For five months we only saw each other on weekends. We communicated mostly by phone and occasionally via e-mail. It seemed that the nights we felt like talking did not coincide. By the time we had our phone conversation at the end of the day, if I was tired, he wanted to talk. If I had time to talk, he was tired and short with me.

One night, when Chuck was first living in Colorado, I called him as I usually did, but he did not answer. I overreacted, first wondering where he was and whom he was with as he had always been reachable. I tried his cell phone and couldn't get him. I got angry and then worried as the hours ticked on and I still could not reach him. My mind conjured up all kinds of worst-case scenarios. When he finally answered, I was in tears. Once I calmed down and we discussed the situation, Chuck agreed that he would keep his cell phone with him and keep it on. I agreed that if I called and he was out having pizza with the other therapists, I would not expect a full report of his day, but I would know where he was and wouldn't worry.

However, we had to plan to make our usual conversations a priority. We had to call each other earlier in the evening. Originally our tendency was to place the call just before turning out the light, but we were too tired by then to share much of what went on in each other's day. As we developed a better pattern, even though I'd never met any of "the boys" he worked with in the residential treatment center, I felt like I knew them almost as well as he did. Because we planned our conversations for when we had more time and were not already half asleep, he was more patient with my babbling on about my day. We were able to stay a part of each other's lives.

Even now, after we have resumed living in the same house, we still have similar issues because I travel and am occasionally on the road for a week or two at a time. The day-to-day communications still take an effort to maintain. We talk on the phone almost every night when I'm gone. I leave notes for Chuck in places I know he will discover them throughout our time apart: in the refrigerator, under his pillow, in a book he is reading, in his organizer, under a few pairs of socks. Sometimes he sends me e-mail. It brightens my day to open up my e-mail while I am on the road and see that I have a note from Chuck.

While these ideas may sound trivial, they go a long way in helping us feel connected. If you are in a commuter marriage—either living apart or with one spouse traveling—I would encourage you to be sure that you are communicating on at least this level before moving on to address deeper issues that may exist.

Get a Heart Check-Up

Meanwhile, anyone in Joan's position needs to be sure that his or her heart is right, fighting any potential anger or resentment. If a person attempts to address concerns with the offending spouse while full of anger, the attempts are apt to backfire and may drive him or her further away. Perhaps this is why talking has not been effective. Gaylen Larson, PhD, warns Joan—and anyone in a similar situation,

> You need to understand the principle that anger feeds anger. If you approach John in an angry manner, you will feed his anger, resulting in a negative outcome. Proverbs says a soft answer turns away anger, and that an angry answer feeds anger (Prov. 15:1). What you want to do is to dispel the anger, not feed it.

To dispel anger effectively, the spouse who sees the need for improvement has to be willing to make the first changes. For example, Joan could begin to make some personal changes through her time with the Lord. Without evening family responsibilities, she has plenty of time to look at her own life and the issues that may be impacting her responses. Addressing similar concerns in her own life, Shirley says,

Although I was deeply involved in speaking and women's ministry, the lack of togetherness began to take its toll. I could feel myself moving toward a depression, so I began to journalize my feelings. I recall getting up one morning at three and going downstairs to write my thoughts to God. I was very honest with Him—since God already knows my heart. I asked Him to help me understand and accept Nate for who and what he is—a good provider, a man of high integrity, a man who I know loves me (in his own way)—and to help me support him in the areas of his needs. The Lord helped me find a good Christian friend who would listen in confidence to my complaints, but would not allow me to tear Nate down or wallow in my self-pity. She listened, empathized with me, and then challenged me with ways to help understand and accept his work and his ways—to love extravagantly, though she did not use that term.

Now I pray for Nate, and I encourage all wives to do the same for their husband. I'd start by reading *The Power of a Praying Wife*, by Stormie Omartian and Marita's book *The Praying Wives Club*—maybe even start or join one in her community. Another book that helped me is *Personality Plus*, by Florence Littauer. Understanding the Personalities and his "work" mode versus her "friend/social" mode would be extremely helpful to anyone in Joan and John's place as it was for Nate and me.

Make Homecomings Special

As addressed above, once you have given the problem to God, made the mental adjustment from anger to understanding, and begun to accept your mate for who he or she is—focusing on the good points—next, I encourage you to be sure that home is a place where your spouse feels welcome and wanted.

In our marriage, I am the one who is often on the road. But as with Joan, Chuck doesn't like that I travel. However, traveling has been a part of my life for all my adult years. When I met Chuck, I was teaching seminars all over the country. I think he should be used to it after twenty-two years of marriage. Instead, he likes it less and less. Since I do not have the financial freedom to change, and Chuck agrees that my speaking and writing is what God has called me to do, I have learned to adjust my travel schedule to work better for our lives.

Like Joan, I am the one who was unhappy with the way things were, I was the one who wanted a change. Coming home on the plane, I often enjoy the relaxing escape of a Christian romance novel. As I read, I picture Chuck meeting me at the gate with roses in his hand. Or, at least dropping what he is doing when I walk in the door to hug me, kiss me, and confirm how much he has missed me.

In reality, the plane lands and I walk alone through the terminal, get my baggage, and go to my car. I wait in line to pay for parking and drive home. Because I like to get home from a trip as soon as possible, I frequently arrive late at night rather than the next day. Chuck is often asleep when I get home. I tiptoe in, drop my bags, and undress in the dark. I crawl into bed beside him and he wiggles his toes against my leg to welcome me home. Hardly the romance novel scene I had painted in my mind.

A few years ago, I was scheduled to fly home the day after a seminar, the day of our anniversary. Since it was our anniversary, I really wanted that romance novel scene. The day before, I had arranged to have flowers sent to Chuck's office with a card that said, "Happy Anniversary! Hurry home!" (I had the flowers delivered in the morning in case he forgot what day it was. They would remind him, and he'd have time to do whatever he needed to do.) I planned to arrive home before he got off work. I had time to shop for the ingredients to make a lovely dinner. I got home, did the dinner prep work, and put it all aside. In the bedroom I found something small and black hanging on our four-poster bed with an anniversary card. (He hadn't forgotten after all.) I relaxed in a bubble bath and put my present on. I lit candles in the bedroom and put something bubbly in the silver bucket next to the bed with two crystal flutes. It was nearly time for him to get home. I crawled up on the bed and read my romance novel. I waited. The dogs barked and I heard his car door. I tucked the romance novel away and placed myself artfully across the bed. I could write my own romance novel with the results of my efforts—and it would not be publishable in the Christian market!

As I reflect on that evening, I realize I put several changes into play.

I had sent Chuck flowers, so he knew that I had not forgotten what day it was. He knew I'd be waiting, and he knew what he had waiting for me. He was excited to see me, glad I had come home. While the night left me breathless, I thought it through the next morning. That was the reaction I'd like to get every time I come home!

Romans 12:18 tells me that it is my job to "live at peace with everyone" (NIV). It does not tell me to change my husband. I thought, "What could I change that would bring about the desired effect?" First, I could change my schedule so I come home before him, instead of after he was asleep. I could fix a special dinner. I could put on one of the many "little somethings" he has given me over the years, and I could place myself across the bed as if in a lingerie catalog. Yes, I could do that. My next trip I did. It worked again—even without the special day and without the flowers. My next trip I tried it again. It worked again. I had created an attitude adjustment. While he is still not crazy about my traveling, he loves my coming home. Without travel, I wouldn't be putting forth the homecoming effort. (I do not go through my "attitude adjustment" routine every time I come home. If I did, it would lose the sense of surprise that makes it special.)

While I doubt that a person in John's place would be expecting a romance-novel greeting—they would probably appreciate the effort. Joan, or anyone in her circumstance, can make some adjustments to be sure he feels welcome, giving him a sense of excitement and enthusiasm about coming home. On the nights that he gets home early enough, she might prepare his favorite meal and serve it in front of the fireplace. When his arrival hour is late, she could try my routine—spending time pampering herself with a bubble bath (or whatever works for her) and getting in the right frame of mind. As Shirley suggests, make his homecomings special:

> I believe that in cases like Joan and John's, if the wife begins to accept her husband just as he is and lets him know that she appreciates his being such a good provider and acknowledges to him that "traveling all the time must be hard on him," and then asks what she can do to make his homecomings special, she will begin to see a difference in their relationship.

Discuss Your Concerns with a Counselor if Necessary

By following Shirley's advice and my example, anyone in Joan's place will be creating an environment that is conducive to discussing other concerns: their limited time together and unmet needs. Then she can ask her husband what his thoughts are and what he sees might take place to remedy the situation. (Of course, in your house, the roles could be reversed.)

By this point, the traveling or absent spouse should be willing to discuss the concerns and make some changes. For example, John must recognize his role as a husband is more than just bringing home a paycheck and playing spouse for a night.

Another peer, Gene, who travels for his job as well, advises,

> John must find balance in his schedule. If a conversation does not resolve the problem, then they should make an appointment to visit a marriage counselor.

Once a couple discusses the issues that are present in their marriage—whether on their own or with a counselor helping them—and have opened up the lines of communication, they can then address the next concern: spending time together.

Creative Time Together

The presenting problem shows that Joan and John have fallen into a trap many couples face, traveling spouse or not. Their relationship has a routine and lacks excitement, variety, and a creative use of time together—which is especially important due to the limited time available. If this rings true in your marriage, read on. These creative, real-life suggestions may be just what you need.

Looking at our case history, we see that while John is working very hard and providing for Joan, the first change he must make is to draw some boundaries and make Joan a priority on the weekends—since they both have this time off. Perhaps this is an adjustment needed at your house as well.

Sometimes when I travel, I am gone weekdays, other times weekends—occasionally both. When Chuck is off weekends and I am home, I make it a policy that my weekends are his. I do not make any plans until I know what he wants to do. Once in a while he wants to go for a bike ride with his friends or build something with a buddy. On those days, I do my projects. Otherwise, I do whatever he wants. He may be involved in a project—which allows me to do mine, such as working on a book—but if he calls for help, I drop what I am doing and go help him. While I think I am letting him know he is my priority, this is something I continually have to work on. Recently, I was on a book deadline. I really wanted to stay focused and write. He asked if I'd like to go on a "picnic" (code for an outdoor romantic interlude). Unfortunately I said, "No," I wanted to keep on track on the book deadline. It was not a happy moment and I spent so long trying to convince him that he was my priority—not the book—that I could have gone on the picnic. Since then, when he suggests any activity on the weekend, I have remembered to enthusiastically agree. Because I am gone so much these days, I need to keep Chuck's needs a priority when I am home.

Chuck's schedule is often extremely varied. Some weeks he has had to work seven days in a row. If I am on a book deadline, I appreciate the fact that he is distracted. One time, when I was writing, he found out at the last minute that he would have the next day off. My natural reaction was to say that I could not play with him that day, as I had to write. Then I realized, "What good is writing a book on marriage if my own marriage is not my priority?" Fortunately, I am self-employed and have the freedom to put my writing aside and took the day off—so I did! We slept in, got out of bed around eleven, had a late breakfast, and went rollerblading for three hours. We went to lunch around 3:30 and took a sunset motorcycle ride that evening. Chuck appreciated that I made him my priority and spent the day with him doing whatever he wanted.

In our case history, John needs to do the same thing for Joan. Since his weekdays, and part of the weekend, don't involve Joan, he needs to make some sacrifices for his marriage. If John makes this adjustment, spending more time with Joan, they can probably reach an agreement that would allow John to golf with his buddies once or twice a month, with Joan getting the other Sundays.

Even if John does not change his priorities and carve out more time to spend with Joan, the time they do have needs to be more creative and stimulating to both of them. Gene says,

> Rather than follow the same routine every week, they need to explore some new activities. Joan needs to arrange a Saturday evening to attend a play or a concert, visit a museum, or spend a romantic evening together at a favorite restaurant.

For couples suffering from a lack of time together, Chuck suggests that they take turns making the decision on how they will spend whatever time they do have together. Once the activity has been decided upon, both must agree to go for it with full enthusiasm. For example, Joan may enjoy the symphony more than John—many women do. So she might select that for their evening out. John needs to go without complaining and make the best of it. Likewise, Joan needs to go to a football game enthusiastically if that is something John might choose to do.

I enjoy going to our symphony's performances, but I especially enjoy them when they are outdoors. Chuck is okay with the symphony, but he really dislikes any activity that is indoors and likes almost anything that is outdoors. Four times a year the New Mexico Symphony plays outside at the zoo. The attire is casual and people bring a blanket or chairs and sit on the lawn with a picnic. These outdoor concerts are a good compromise for us. To make it extra special, I prepare a terrific picnic menu and pack everything. Chuck gets out the red wagon and we load it all into the car. At the zoo our little red wagon attracts a lot of admiration as Chuck pulls it to a grassy spot loaded with the chairs, blanket, picnic basket, and cooler. We agree that lying under the stars listening to Gershwin is about as perfect as a summer evening gets.

Chuck does the symphony for me. I go on motorcycle rides for him. For several years, he had a Harley Sportster. If that means anything to you, you know it is not a comfortable bike for long rides. His had a little button-like seat on the back fender for passengers. When we go for longer rides through the mountains to a famous motorcyclist hangout for lunch, I find myself hanging on and praying, "Oh God, help me have a good attitude." For Chuck's fiftieth birthday, he wants to fly to California, rent a Harley (one that is comfortable) in Los Angeles and spend a few days driving up the coast on Highway One. We'll use my frequent flyer points for airfare and lodging and make the trek.

For Chuck's birthday one year, I wanted to do something very different. I had been on the road and was scheduled to come home in the middle of the day on his birthday. I thought about throwing a surprise party. But his Perfect Melancholy personality doesn't go for that sort of thing. Have some friends over for dinner? But Chuck has been working such long hours, I knew he would not want to be in an "up" mood for a bunch of people, plus his birthday fell on a work night. I had to think of what would be special for him. I know Chuck likes picnics, and his work schedule has prevented us from having many this summer, so that is what I planned.

I had "happy birthday" flowers sent to him at work telling him to hurry home. I got home in time to prepare a lovely picnic dinner: grilled chicken Caesar salad with a croissant and a bubbly beverage, and fresh brownies for dessert. I packed it all up with our portable picnic table. A friend took me up to the top of the Petroglyphs (cliffs overlooking the city of Albuquerque) where I set up the picnic, arranging his presents around the table. I had left a card with a riddle at home for Chuck. When solved, he would know where to meet me. As soon as we saw Chuck driving toward the Petroglyphs, my friend left. I was alone when Chuck got there. We ate dinner and watched the sunset in one direction and the lights of the city come on in the other. We had a lovely evening! We agreed that we needed to do that more often.

Couples who have to be apart frequently, need to plan special activities together. Take into consideration what you like to do together and individually. In Joan and John's case, perhaps Joan could learn to golf so John can still golf, but they could be together—or she could drive the cart. Think of your marriage. There are bound to be things you know your spouse would like to do.

To prevent falling into a rut, try one of the many books available that offer creative dates for couples. Simply entering the word "dating" on Amazon.com brought up over 100,000 books. Two I suggest are by Dave and Claudia Arp: *10 Dates to Revitalize Your Marriage* and *52*

Dates for You and Your Mate. Pick up one of these books and spend an evening selecting a few dates that you both agree sound like fun.

Make God the Center of Your Marriage

Another issue of concern found in the presenting problem is that it appears Joan and John do not have any spiritual connection. Church attendance should be one of the activities that all couples do together as our Christian life offers the foundation for the marriage commitment. Seek out a church with worship services offered on Saturday night as well as Sunday. The option of attending on Saturday can leave Sunday morning open for personal quality time—something a commuter marriage lacks. While this may sound somewhat heretical to some, I think God would honor the decision to encourage a healthy marital relationship.

Consider Changes

Even after Joan and John—or you and your spouse—work together to improve communication, talk about concerns, and spend creative time together, they may find that they are still suffering from lack of time together. In fact, once they really start to enjoy each other again, they may find that they both resent John's traveling even more. Since Joan is a schoolteacher she may be able to join John on some of his trips during the summer.

Jo, one of our peer advisors with a similar marriage situation, traveled with her husband Ray from time to time. From her experience, she says:

> We tried to work it out so that I could go with Ray occasionally, but Ray eventually decided he missed being with me more than he enjoyed the prestigious title and the hectic schedule it required. When an opportunity to change positions presented itself, Ray took it in order to cut back on travel time. He was highly respected in his industry, and when he answered the question about why he took a demotion in his career, he

answered truthfully, "To spend less time on the road and more time with my wife. Our relationship is more important than anything." Every man hearing that has told Ray they admire him for doing it. We are thoroughly enjoying having more time together.

While all traveling men or women won't look at the situation as Ray did, they do need to value the feelings and insight of their marriage partner and respond with care and love. Chuck and I lived in different states for five months. I drove back and forth most weekends. We tried hard to make it work. But it is very difficult to have a marriage when weekends are all you have together.

Many couples live apart long-term. Others make it through a few months of a temporary situation. Whichever your case, I hope the insights offered here will help you love each other extravagantly—to give, not to get.

The Interactions

For couples in a similar situation to John and Joan, Chuck would assign the following "homework" assignment:

1. Create a balance sheet on the traveling spouse's job to determine if it is worth the strain on the marriage. In separate columns, list the costs and benefits of the current job. This will help you see in black and white whether or not to stay in this job.
2. Each spouse should ask him or herself, "If things remain exactly the same, how long do I think I can hang in there?" Then share the responses. This is an indicator of how critical the situation is and how urgent the need for change. Different solutions to the problem require more time to complete than others. When time is short, bold action is required.
3. Depending on the answers to the previous exercises, begin to look for avenues for change. For example, if both agree that a job change is not needed, what changes can be made in the weekend routine? List specific variations and select one for each upcoming

weekend. Even if a job change is agreed upon, it may take months to implement. Therefore a change in the weekend routine may still be needed.
4. Because of the minimal time you have together, maximize the time that you do have. Schedule time weekly—about an hour—to do The Couple's Communication Exercise (see app. C). It will be especially valuable to this situation.

Six

Rocky Roads

Job Loss, Change in Life Direction

The Issue

It was the second marriage for both Rich and Pat. If their expectations for their first marriage had been high, now, they had bet the farm. They were older, more mature; the children from their first marriages were grown and off on their own. They had promised to love each other's offspring, make them welcome in their new home, and never belittle the children's other parent. They were aware that their divorces had forced their children into new, strange, and frightening circumstances.

It would be just the two of them, working on their lives together, going forward with their hopes and dreams. They knew something of their mistakes, were somewhat aware of their shortcomings, and had resolved that nothing would destroy what they had found together. They had moved to a new city to rebuild their lives, leaving everything behind to start anew. Knowing that they needed something "greater than themselves," they had committed their lives to the Lord and found an ideal church for worship. There they had "family," felt nourished, and made friends. It seemed everything was in place—at least for a while.

Both Rich and Pat were professionals. Pat was an editor for a major magazine, and Rich, a corporate executive. Their careers were on track, money was not a problem—they were secure in their future, one another, and the Lord.

However, a coup in Rich's organization created a big bump in the road. He, along with the CEO and other top executives, were thrown out. Rich has a wide range of experience and thought that getting another position would not be a problem—even if it took awhile. He hadn't anticipated that his age, now fifty-five, would make it difficult. He hadn't acknowledged that the business world had become a "younger place." In the months since his job loss, no career opportunities have come his way. Rich has tired of being "over qualified." He is angry and scared from the inside out. Nothing in his life has any of the familiar signposts. The world has become a strange and frightening place for him.

Rich is beginning to realize that he has always staked his life on his abilities. His career, position, power, and influence defined him, gave him his identity and respectability. He has competed in the corporate marketplace and provided for his family. Now, it seems that his abilities no longer count.

While Rich has been struggling, Pat's magazine position suddenly came to an abrupt end. Although she has been a career person, she always thought there would be a husband who would take care of her and see to her needs. After all, hadn't her dad done just that? She didn't expect the road to be this rocky.

With neither of them bringing in any income, they have resorted to selling off property and investments—netting far less than their original value, thus hastening more and more sell off. Now, there is nothing left.

Desperate, Rich has taken a job in a discount warehouse. The pay is a far cry from what he has known and had assumed would always be there.

Rich seems to be unable to talk with Pat about any of their circumstances or his fear and shame over this turn of events in their lives. When Pat tries to talk about what is happening to them, Rich cannot. When Pat insists, Rich becomes angry and shuts her out. Pat feels isolated, confused, and sick at heart about this turn of events in their lives. But more so, that she and Rich don't seem to be partners any longer. She finds she distances herself from her husband and seeks her own way in activities that further separate them.

The Insights

Many of us in a modern marriage can relate to Rich and Pat's story. Often couples seem to do well when life is cruising along, but when the difficulties crash upon them, underlying issues come to the surface. With the instability of today's job market, men and women who thought their career path was firm, find themselves in a position similar to Rich and Pat. To ensure that the insight offered here will be helpful to many couples, we will look primarily at job loss and a change of lifestyle.

Job Loss

Find Your Worth in Christ

While some women face a similar situation, Rich's predicament is very typical of men today—their security and worth is centered in their profession. However, as Christians we all need to find our value in life in Christ; work does not define the believer.

With an understanding of how Rich feels, Charles offers peer insight from his experience. Charles and his wife, Karen, faced similar circumstances when a company reshuffle caused him to lose his position as a CFO in a major insurance company at the age of fifty-nine. Charles says of that time in his life:

> My greatest fear was that I could no longer depend on myself. Hard work and experience now made no difference. Success and accomplishment eluded me. I had "worshiped" at those altars all my life. It was all I knew; it was what made me worthy.

When Charles's self worth was in question, he pulled away from

Karen and isolated himself, taking his anger at the world out on her. Many times Karen found herself reminding Charles that she was not the enemy. As Charles pushed her away, she had to do things on her own. She took up hiking and camping. She got some counsel, and she grew—all the while being patient with Charles as he dealt with his fears. During this time, Charles took a job as a night manager at a gas station where he had previously been a customer. His time of transition included driving a laundry truck, selling shoes, and managing a clothing store's shoe department.

As Karen grew, Charles realized that if he wanted to "keep up" with her, he needed to make some changes as well. Finally he turned to Christian counseling and got involved in a men's Bible study. Charles says,

> It wasn't long before I saw that my worth was caught up in my corporate image. It was time to lean on the Lord as never before. Now, it seemed the Lord was instructing me that obedience to His directives was my business; the outcome of my endeavors was His. He would teach me that being smart, having power, prestige, and position had kept me from Him. He showed me that He would allow hurt and pain, failure and guilt, confusion and remorse to attack me so that finally there would be no place for me to go but to Him.

A few years ago, Chuck and I faced something similar as well. Economics in the healthcare profession caused Chuck to take a job in sales much below his expectations and education. He liked to say his position as a car salesman was "taking a mental health break from mental health" and he was able to earn a good living selling Jaguars. (He has always loved Jaguars and has owned one most of his life.) While waiting for customers at the car dealership, he had time to read through the entire New Testament. In doing so, God showed him that work is just work. Chuck saw that the apostle Paul was a tentmaker—though his education and position as a Pharisee would indicate that he could have had a much more prestigious position. Prior to his encounter with Christ, we can assume that Paul held an authoritative post within the

Jewish community. Yet the Bible does not talk much about Paul's profession, but more about his actions and how he changed the world after his conversion. The Personality Profile for Paul in the *Life Application Study Bible* says, "No person, apart from Jesus himself, shaped the history of Christianity like the apostle Paul."[1]

Charles and Chuck were Christians when life dealt them a hard blow. For both of them, it was in that downtime that their relationship with Christ grew to a new level, to a place where they could view their job as just that—a job, like tentmaking. It does not define who they are.

While it is easier said than done, the first step Chuck advises Rich—or anyone in a situation similar to his—to take, is to adjust his thinking about his worthiness. For example, Rich's job at the discount warehouse is just a job, a way to bring in some income, but it does not define who he is.

Center on Christ

Gaylen Larson, PhD, sees that Rich is struggling with self-esteem issues from which he feels like he will never recover. As a result, Gaylen sees that,

> Because men define their worth by what they do, it would be important for Pat to go overboard in complimenting him. It may also help if he would teach a class at church or be involved in some leadership position. Even participating in a small group can be a great way to find support, love, and friendship. With a group that is based on Christ, healing can take place. These are ideas to help him feel better about himself.

Once a person struggling with issues like Rich's reaches this place and allows his relationship with Christ to take on a deeper meaning in his life, he can then begin to see his marriage as a three-way relationship between him, his wife, and God. Charles tells of this time in his life:

> God taught me that my relationship with Karen was a direct barometer of how my relationship was with Him. Now, I mar-

vel at what the Lord has given us in our marriage. It is simply sweet. It is far beyond what I had thought would be possible for us, or for any marriage. As it is in all things, this marriage is His, not mine, not Karen's—but I am sure glad I am one of the participants!

Build Communication with Each Other

After a change in one's thinking about security and a relationship with Christ, Chuck next advises that couples in this place need to begin to build communication and open up to their true feelings. Maxine Marsolni, author of *Blended Families,* offers couples facing this shift in security this counsel:

> When life throws you a curve ball—and you should expect it will once in a while, come together in prayer and goal attainment. So many of us seem to tie our sense of worth to our pocketbook and not our core personhood set forth by our creator. Until a couple can talk about their true feelings, it will be difficult to overcome the shame that accompanies their unmet expectations. Humility is often a hard ball to grasp, yet is the very core element of Christianity and marital bliss.

For Charles and Karen, prayer was an important part of the restoration of their relationship as well. Charles reflects,

> We began to pray together each morning—walking and talking. Then we came together to discuss finances, future goals, and decisions that would affect our children.

As Charles was rediscovering himself in Christ, he was able to talk to Karen about what he was learning. Karen welcomed his conversations and encouraged him. Eventually, they recommitted themselves to the Lord, to one another, and to their family.

Our case history mentions Pat's expectations: while she planned to work, she also thought she would have a husband who would be there to take care of her. As we will discuss in the "Career Chaos" chapter, the reality today is that women need to let go of that expectation. Jobs are no longer secure, and a couple needs to work together. This is one of the ways that the love extravagantly concept can be put into practice. For example, Pat needs to let go of her expectations and anger toward Rich for not being there for her in her time of need—"not to get, but to give." True love, extravagant love, is helping each other, supporting each other, and esteeming each above the other.

Change in Life Direction

The Shrug

Help on attitude adjustment came for Chuck in some entertaining armchair travel books by Peter Mayle: *A Year in Provence, Toujours Provence,* and *Encore Provence.* In these books, Peter Mayle introduces a French habit he calls the "classic Gaelic shrug," a physical habit that means so much more. He describes it this way:

> A certain amount of limbering-up is required before any major body parts are brought into action, and your first moves should be nothing more than a frown and a slight sideways tilt of the head. These indicate that you cannot believe the foolishness, the impertinence, or the plain dumb ignorance of what the Parisian has just said to you. There is a short period of silence before the Parisian tries again, repeating this remark and looking at you with some degree of irritation. Maybe he thinks you're deaf, or Belgian and therefore confused by his sophisticated accent. Whatever he feels, you now have his complete attention. This is the moment to demolish him and his nonsense with a flowing, unhurried series of movements as the full shrug is unfurled.

> Step One.   The jaw is pushed out as the mouth is turned down.

Step Two. The eyebrows are fully cocked and the head comes forward.

Step Three. The shoulders are raised to earlobe level, the elbows tucked in to the side, the hands fanning out with palms facing upward.

Step Four. (optional) You allow a short, infinitely dismissive sound—something between flatulence and a sigh—to escape from your lips before letting the shoulders return to a resting position.

It might almost be a yoga exercise, and I must have seen it hundreds of times. It can be used to signify disagreement, disapproval, resignation, or contempt, and it effectively terminates any discussion. As far as I know, there is no countershrug, or satisfactory answering gesture. For these reasons, it is an invaluable gesture for anyone like myself whose command of the French language is far from perfect. A well-timed shrug speaks volumes.[2]

With the body language of the shrug, the person says, "Oh well. Life goes on." Chuck suggests that anyone coming to terms with a disappointing direction in life practice this cognitive process by pairing the physical action—palms turned out, elbows pointed out, corners of the mouth turned down, with the mental letting go/letting God idea. Chuck has been working on making this behavior modification in his own life. Rather than getting upset or being too hard on himself, Chuck is learning to shrug. Sometimes he will just look at me and say, "Shrug." He is learning to let go and would advise Rich, for example, to do the same thing.

Look for New Opportunities

If, like Rich, you are facing a new life direction, Chuck asks you to consider, "Is God preparing both of you for something new? Should you start a business or ministry together? Do something with e-commerce or go back to school?" Capitalize on your experience by "mining" the treasures. This may take the form of writing an article in a business magazine, a Web site support group for displaced executives, or a how-to booklet on avoiding the unexpected pitfalls in business. Often community colleges hire executives and other experts to teach business classes at night. Find some outlet for giving of yourself—possibly in a mentorship capacity, volunteer a few hours a month in an area of your interests. Not only will this help others, it could help curb self-pity and go far to gaining a new, healthier view of yourself. When people start to feel better about themselves, it seems that the rest of life tends to line up and gravitate toward more positive experiences.

Many people have chosen to leave the corporate rat race and make a different life for themselves. In Rich and Pat's case, and maybe yours, perhaps God has made the choice for them. Shrug—and move on. Think about what new directions God may have for you.

In reading about Rich and Pat, Jan and Carl offer these peer insights:

> Our situation was similar, except that we both chose to leave the corporate world—which meant severe downsizing and adapting a mindset of simplifying life so we had more time to pursue our passions and serve the Lord. It has brought on struggles for which we were not prepared, and we are constantly re-examining our priorities, life mission, and how we define ourselves. As two separate people bringing in two paychecks, it is easy to be independent, but downsizing forces interdependence and sacrifice, needs versus wants, and a complete change in lifestyle.

While the practical reality was far more complicated than the dream of carrying it out, Jan and Carl report that they would not trade their situation for the way it was. From their experience, they offer hope to anyone in this place.

> Look for the blessing in being free of the corporate jungle. See God's hand in this change. Jobs, like Rich's at the warehouse, are only a stopgap measure to bring in some groceries. Indi-

vidually, each spouse should find out what God is calling them to do and do it—no matter what the salary. Sell the big house, if you have one, and live in what you can afford. Couples, like Rich and Pat, who are both healthy and still young have no reason for poverty. Without the trappings, they will find greater meaning in life!

The Interactions

For couples in a similar situation to Rich and Pat, Chuck would assign the following "homework" assignment:

1. Using The Couple's Communication Exercise (see app. C), talk through your fears with one another. In a written format, list the worst case scenario for the coming months. What is the worst that could happen? Flip the paper over (indicating two sides of the coin) and write out the best case scenario, all the good that could come in spite of financial losses. This exercise should draw the two of you together. Additionally, after completing the assignment you would see that much of the situation is under your control. You have a choice to make the best or the worst of these circumstances.
2. It is a mistake for people to identify themselves strictly with their current job. Individually, write out what you each see as your own self-identity, listing all the things that make up who you are. Think of what you would want your grandchildren to remember about each of you. This will help remove your focus from the unimportant (your profession) and on to the enduring.

. . . So all their work is useless, like chasing the wind. (Ecclesiastes 2:26 NCV)

3. Set common and personal goals for growth. For example, a couple might decide to spend one hour a day in Bible study, choose to work on their physical health by spending time in exercise together, or learn to cook. This shift from career focus will allow

you more time for personal growth. Working toward achieving these goals will keep you from dwelling on the negative while making good use of the available time.
4. Independently, each spouse should write out their expectations of the other during this trying time. Then come together and discuss them, agreeing upon changes that each is willing to make to meet the other's expectations. Some expectations may prove to be valid; others will need to be thrown out once they are verbalized. Once the expectations are clear and agreed upon, resentment, hostility, and anger toward one another will be minimized.

Seven

Sacrificed Her Career

Personal Fulfillment, Career Options

The Issue

Troy was a high-powered salesman, flying half a million miles a year—gathering up frequent flyer tickets the way that some people collect grocery coupons. A gregarious Powerful Choleric with some Perfect Melancholy, Troy had a massive stroke six and a half years ago. He was fifty-six. Annette, his Popular Sanguine/Powerful Choleric wife, was forty-six. While originally completely debilitated, Troy has progressed from a wheelchair, to a cane, and now to walking—although his left leg still drags a bit. Together Troy and Annette have worked their way back to a halfway "normal" life.

The first three years after Troy's stroke, Annette was Troy's primary caregiver. She had to quit her job because she couldn't leave him long enough to go to work. The stroke caused him to do things that were unsafe—he'd leave the water running or the gas stove on. But he finally got beyond that, began to drive, and now pretty much functions as he had before. He has lost the use of his left arm, but manages to compensate.

Around year four, people began to ask Annette why she didn't get a job. With neither of them working, their income went from over

$100,000 a year to less than $35,000 from disability insurance. They could use an extra income. Annette's self-image began to suffer as they continued living on the disability payments, and she missed the intellectual stimulation her job had provided.

One of the things that attracted Annette to Troy was the power that came from his position. He was strong, and together they had an enviable lifestyle. Now after six and a half years of disability, Troy no longer has the same magnetism he once did. While Annette has stood by his side and supported him through the difficulties, she is concerned about going back into the work force. Her effervescent nature has always attracted men, especially those who want to take care of her. Annette feels empty. She is afraid if a man paid any attention to her, it would be too great a temptation—she might up and run away! However, she loves her husband and as a Christian feels she should not put herself in what could be a compromising position. So, she's remained at home—waiting for the Lord to show her a better idea.

The stroke and its aftermath created an extreme shift in the marriage—Annette and Troy need a new equilibrium. Annette wants to continue to grow. Her husband now looks old to her and she still feels young! She believes she sacrificed her career to save her marriage. However, Annette is now in a place where she can do something that uses her skills and abilities while giving her the mental and emotional stimulation she longs for.

The Insights

While Troy and Annette's situation presents her need for a job and her fear of temptation as primary concerns, we see a bigger issue. This is common to many women, no matter how healthy their husbands may be—expecting her husband to fulfill all of her needs and interests. If Annette addresses this first, her career options and the temptation they provide will be less of a worry. Additionally, she needs to deal with the underlying anger she feels over her unbalanced sacrifice. We'll also look at some things Troy can do to help the situation.

Personal Fulfillment

Annette's personality is the combination of the Popular Sanguine/Powerful Choleric. This tells us she likes lots of activity and stimulation. Additionally, we know that Annette is ten years younger than Troy. So, while Troy is ready to slow down and retire—possibly even if he had no disability—Annette still desires more activity. As women often marry older men, this is a situation that may be present in your marriage even if there is no health issue.

Annette is to be commended for honoring her marriage vows and sticking with Troy through the past six years. Being a caregiver is not a position that her personality type would naturally gravitate toward. Now, however, Annette says that she is running on empty. This is natural in her place. For over six years she has been doing nothing that fills her or stimulates her. Her whole life has been focused around her husband and caring for him—she has been giving extravagant love.

Fortunately for Annette, she can now make some changes. Unlike a terminally or chronically ill person, Troy no longer needs constant care. If your situation today is that of being a caregiver, either long-term or temporary, you need something that will offer you emotional and spiritual nourishment to fill you up—or like Annette, you will find that you are running on empty.

As I talk to women around the country, I find that many women expect their husbands to fulfill all their needs: physical, emotional, and spiritual. If he isn't their provider, best friend, spiritual leader, and companion in shared activities, they feel disappointed and cheated. I believe it is unreasonable to expect any one human being to meet all our needs. In her book *The Power of Femininity,* Michelle McKinney Hammond says, "We will strive, weep, and deprive ourselves of opportunities to live a full life if we put our hope in a person to fulfill our expectations."[1]

Check Your Spiritual Walk

First, many of our needs can only be met through an ongoing and active relationship with our Lord, Jesus Christ. So, I would ask anyone in a situation that bears any of the elements of Annette's, "How is your spiritual walk? Are you in a women's Bible study group, one that offers you both spiritual food and fellowship?" Because the fellowship aspect is so important for Annette as she finds a new equilibrium in her marriage, I believe a group study is a vital link for her. She could read the Bible or use a study guide on her own. Both of these activities would be beneficial, but a group study also offers much-needed social interaction.

To find out about Bible study groups in the area, start with the women's ministries in your own church, then call some of the major churches near you home, or check with the local Christian bookstore. Christian bookstores often know of Bible study groups because they have ordered supplies for them or because they have postings of Christian activities. Another option is to look in the local newspaper's religion section (usually on Saturday) that lists events taking place within the community.

In addition, all Christian couples should consider studying the Bible together—either a couples' group study or just the two of them. Maxine Marsolini, author of *Blended Families,* recommends a study called *Becoming One* by Don Meridith. Maxine says,

> It is a great study to do because it moves life's trials away from selfish feelings into an enjoyable and focused Extravagant Love commitment.

Make Some Friends

Attending a group study will help anyone in Annette's place fill both her spiritual and social needs. For a Popular Sanguine, like Annette, her need for friendship cannot be ignored. Consequently, I'd encourage Annette to seek other forms of social activity with female friends as well. If you are in a similar situation, ask yourself, "Is there a physical activity I enjoy, or have enjoyed in the past?" In my area, the local bike store hosts a women's ride every Wednesday evening. I have enjoyed joining them occasionally for a casual ride along the river. Many gyms host aerobics classes or other group activities that would provide you with a forum for meeting women your age and with similar interests. Taking a class through the community college or other adult education programs would be another option. A woman in Annette's circumstance needs to develop a social network of friends who can encourage her and lift her up. After being a caretaker for an extended time, you may find many of your former friends have moved on. Or, your previous social network might have been largely related to her work. Get out and make new friends!

Have Fun!

Another way to fill one's emotional tank and prevent the running-on-empty feeling is with activities you enjoy. Surely, some of these activities are things that can be done without your disabled spouse. You can also explore other avenues.

Even for someone who does not have a spouse with a handicap, this is good advice. For example, I like to sail. Chuck does not enjoy it the same way I do. He would rather ride his bike. Since sailing is not something I can easily do all by myself, I gave it up for a while. I found that I was harboring resentment toward Chuck because he did not join in this activity with me. Then I realized it is unrealistic to expect Chuck to share every activity with me or for me to expect Chuck to meet 100 percent of my needs. One day our newspaper had a feature on a local sailing club that holds races on the lakes here in New Mexico. For a while, I joined. I love the feeling of standing on the bow with the wind in my hair, the sun on my face, and the splash of the refreshing water cooling me off. While I drove three hours each way to get to a lake, this seemed like nothing compared to the satisfaction I receive from the activity. After a while, my life went another direction and the sailing no longer seemed important.

These three areas—spiritual walk, friends, and satisfying activities—will nourish the soul of anyone in Annette's situation and help her feel fulfilled. For those with her personality, these are especially important. By feeling strengthened and stimulated with healthy activities, the temptation to stray will be lessened.

Find New Interests You Can Share

While these insights will help anyone in a care-giving situation, it will do little to restore the marriage's vitality. In Annette's case, Troy is now capable of at least a somewhat normal life; they need to explore things they can do together.

Speaking from her own experience with disability, Helen offers the following peer insight:

> I know firsthand how a serious illness or injury can affect a marriage. Due to an accident, I am also disabled. I encourage Annette, and anyone dealing with similar circumstances to remember that her husband is still the same man she loved and married. While it is a challenge, she can still have a glorious and exciting marriage. If she and her husband can learn to focus on doing everything they can think to do to court and encourage each other, her life will be sweet. Now is the time to test those vows they repeated when they were married. They've made it through the worst part. They can now start rebuilding what was lost. God promises that he will restore the years the locusts have eaten (Joel 2:25). An affair with another man can't compare with the joy she can find right in her own marriage if she will seek ways to build up her husband. If she will crown him her king, he in turn will treat her as his queen. What a payoff! I've experienced restoration in my marriage and it is marvelous.

In an effort to rebuild what was lost, couples like Annette and Troy might try traveling together. Every few months they could plan a special weekend away at a bed and breakfast. They might take a photography class or a gourmet cooking class together. Whatever their interests or level of physical activity, they need to do things together that they can both enjoy. For Annette, loving Troy extravagantly may mean being willing to adjust her faster pace to his new lower key pace. In their new place of equilibrium, the things they did together previously may no longer be possible. Rather than mourn that loss, they can celebrate what they can still do together.

Find an Emotionally Healthy Outlet

If you are facing a situation like Annette and Troy's, after you work to rebuild your life and relationship, look at a couple additional areas. While not mentioned in the given case history, Melanie Wilson, PhD, is concerned that Annette will act irresponsibly if she does not find an outlet for her anger and grief. While Melanie's questions are directed toward Annette, anyone in a similar place can benefit from Melanie's professional insights. She asks,

> Has she expressed her anger through journaling, through prayer, or to her husband? Although she has willingly submitted her own needs to care for her husband (and this is to be praised), she must have some feelings of anger, disappointment, and grief. If she has not worked through these feelings and expressed them openly, trouble could still be brewing. Sharing her anger and grief with her husband and directing it at the stroke (rather than at him), can be healing and restorative. Doing something as simple as writing down the things that the stroke took away from them can be a wonderful exercise. Only when the anger and grief have been expressed can the couple focus on the blessings they still share and the strengths they can capitalize on in the future.

Offering insights as a peer advisor, as the spouse with the disability, Jo agrees with Melanie's advice. Jo says:

> I, too, am disabled. I was married for eight years before being diagnosed with Multiple Sclerosis during my husband's first year in seminary. From the beginning of dealing with the disease, I poured out my fears and struggles to God in my prayer journal. I remember discussing my Scripture search regarding healing with my husband as we prayed for that very thing and did not receive the answer we desired.
>
> God's answer has been, "I will be with you in the midst of MS" and He has done that very thing for over twenty-three

years. I learned to thank Him while dealing with it (1 Thess. 5:18) and thank Him for what He could do in and through it (Eph. 5:20). Praising God for who He is, not what He could do for me became crucial for my spiritual growth (Ps. 92:1–2; 2 Cor. 1:3).

Five years after the diagnosis, my husband, who was a full-time pastor and seminary PhD student, began an affair with a girlfriend of mine. My husband had become bitter and had not dealt with his anger at God, nor me for having MS and for dealing with it so well. His affair lasted over a year and nearly devastated me. Had I not continued clinging to God, I shudder to think what would have become of me. After fifteen years of marriage, my husband left the pastorate, his doctoral studies, and me, then filed for a divorce I didn't want. A year later, he called me. He told me he was sorry for having nearly destroyed me and that he was sorry for dissolving our marriage; however, he did not want to work on it again.

By not dealing with his emotional and spiritual struggles, my husband had let himself see only the MS instead of me. He resented the way our life changed rather than choosing to look for things we could do together.

Four years later a wonderful man took the risk of marrying me and MS. We have had thirteen years of health challenges, ensuing spiritual and emotional growth, and more fun together than some couples ever have! We tandem, because I can't ride a bike alone. We ski—I use helps designed for the disabled. We enjoy traveling and sightseeing, eating out, serving the Lord, Bible study, and worship. We enjoy sitting side-by-side knowing we share a deep love born out of adversity.

Jo is a speaker, singer, and writer. She definitely hasn't let self-pity get the best of her.

While the presenting problem deals with Annette, Chuck has concern for Troy. Chuck would counsel Troy—or any man with a disability—with the following insight:

Stretch yourself, get away from being defined by your disability and redefine yourself with your abilities. I encourage you to connect with other men through work, church, or organizations focused on helping stroke survivors. You need to be as self sufficient as possible, allowing Christian brothers to help when needed. This will help you see Annette as your wife and lover rather than your nursemaid. Expecting her to do both places her in a difficult position.

Career Options

From Annette's comments we get the idea that her interest in returning to the workforce is more from a need for stimulation rather than for money. Yes, the additional income would be beneficial, but not required. Therefore, Annette has some freedom in her occupational choices.

Vicki Jackson, LCSW, suggests that Annette create some type of entrepreneurial home business that would allow her to bring in some income, have intellectual stimulation, and still be at home much of the time. She says:

> Depending on what common interests the couple had prior to the disability, they could consider a business that might involve both of them. She could even write and present workshops through the local hospital about the shift in a relationship that comes when one spouse has an illness or accident. Think creatively, talk to other couples in similar predicaments, ask the Lord for ideas, and review entrepreneur and women's magazines for motivation stories that tell of other women's adversities and how they overcame them.

I couldn't agree more with Vicki's comments. I am a big proponent of women-owned businesses, especially those that are entrepreneurial or home-based in nature. "Celebrate Your Passions," the last chapter in my book *You've Got What It Takes,* would be an excellent resource for Annette or anyone in her position. Additionally, a home-based business would remove Annette's concerns about temptation and infidelity. However, Chuck comments:

> There is temptation everywhere. Rather than remove herself from any possibility of it, Annette will do better to first focus on filling that emptiness she refers to and building up her relationship with Troy.

Look at what you have always wanted to do and take this opportunity to try something new! Work no longer has to control your life. You can continue to grow as individuals as well as growing as a couple with our focus on doing God's will as the foundation of your life together.

All marriages face shifts at one time or another. Many of us face health or career challenges. By being willing to love extravagantly, to give, not to get, Annette and Troy—or you and your spouse—can find a new equilibrium that works for them, their interests, and their unique situation.

The Interactions

For couples in a similar situation to Annette and Troy, Chuck would assign the following "homework" assignment:

1. As mentioned in this chapter, the non-disabled spouse needs to develop interests that will bring personal fulfillment. As one's personal life is nourished, the temptation to stray will be minimized.
2. The wife (husband, depending on the circumstance) needs to begin to rebuild her professional life. Start by brainstorming career options that will provide mental stimulation. Include the potential risks she feels are present in each one. A viable option might be developing a business with her husband.
3. The husband must identify a Christian friend to whom he can be accountable. This person will agree to be his coach, making him stretch to expand his world: someone who will get him moving when he is feeling sorry for himself and applaud him when he has achieved a new goal.

4. The spouse with the disability needs to identify ten new activities or resources to expand his life. These might be written on a dry-erase board where they can be kept in sight and changed as needed. One of them might be to link up with (or create if needed) a support group for stroke victims, for example. Another might be an athletic endeavor; rather than playing golf with the heavy hitters, he might go to the driving range. He might also cultivate friendships with men with similar disabilities. Using a calendar, begin scheduling two new activities a week for four consecutive weeks.
5. The disabled partner needs to prepare a talking paper that he will later present to the wife. In developing this outline of what he will say to his wife face-to-face, he should express his appreciation for the love and care that she has provided during this medical crisis. At the end he will emphasize that he is improving daily and that as he progresses, she is free to begin rebuilding her life, independent of caring for him. This will give her validation for her sacrifice while giving her permission and encouragement to expand her life. Once he has delineated the points he wants to share with his wife, and perhaps reviewing them with his accountability partner, he needs to share his feelings with her.
6. Together husband and wife need to discuss their changing expectations of each other as the relationship takes on a new equilibrium. This should be done on a weekly basis during this period of transition.

Eight

Career Chaos

Job Security, Depression

The Issue

Christine and Steve have been married for thirteen years. It is Steve's second marriage, but Christine's first. They are compatible in many ways and have similar personalities, but in different proportions. He is Powerful Choleric with some Popular Sanguine while Christine is Perfect Melancholy first with a secondary of Powerful Choleric. While they complement each other, Christine is bewildered at how different they are in one big area: the management of their careers. Christine's path has been fairly smooth and steady; Steve's career is extremely chaotic. She absolutely loves what she does and her career has fallen into place very nicely. Steve gets depressed about his business failures.

Steve has had countless jobs in the past thirteen years. He is a salesperson, and he says it's just really hard to find good sales jobs in which you can actually make a living. At the same time, he is a big dreamer with an entrepreneurial spirit. He has tried his hand at numerous ventures, but none have lasted. Sometimes he has launched out on his own, sometimes with a partner. Sometimes he has made a little money; usually he has gotten them deeply into debt. Whenever a business venture fails, he goes to work for some company as a salesperson. Christine is always relieved that he has a steady paycheck coming in again. But it never lasts for long because he always has his eye open for a "better opportunity"—whether that means another job or an entrepreneurial venture. Earlier this year, he even tried his hand at day-trading, believing that to be a relatively easy business he could develop on his own. It wasn't. Again, Steve lost money.

Christine doesn't want Steve to lose his optimism and confidence about finding an "ideal" business situation. However, it wears her out just watching him! The lack of stability is nerve-racking. Steve says, "There's no guarantee of stability even if you've worked for a company for twenty years." Christine thinks, "That may be true, but we'll never know it from firsthand experience!"

She has accepted that Steve is created differently than she is and that he will probably always continue searching for "greener grass" in his career. But she struggles to cope with the constant changes and the lack of security. She has difficulty maintaining the trust and respect a wife desires to have for her husband while keeping a nonjudgmental attitude.

The Insights

With the information given about Steve and Christine, I have chosen to focus on two of their problems that are apt to be most like those you may be facing: lack of job security and the resulting depression. Because job security is usually more important to women, this chapter will explore some practical ways a woman with Christine's concerns can shore up her sense of security. Additionally, we will address how she can support her husband in dealing with this situational depression.

Job Security

Christine has taken a big step in accepting that after a thirteen-year history, Steve will probably always make frequent job changes. While she can accept this intellectually, it is harder to take to heart on an emotional level. As she states, she still struggles with the "constant changes and lack of security."

Vicki Jackson, LCSW, agrees that Christine is wise in realizing that she cannot change Steve, but encourages Christine to make some changes in her attitude and behavior. On a practical level, Vicki suggests that since Christine's employment is solid and stable, they should consider putting aside a nest egg to cushion the financial reverses caused by her husband's uncertain career path. Additionally, she'd advise Christine and Steve to set specific financial goals, possibly even hiring a financial planner to help them communicate their desires about what they expect from each other in matters of finance and security in their relationship. This will give Christine more security and allow her to be less judgmental of Steve's frequent job changes. Vicki believes that when Steve sees this change in Christine, he may be less defensive and resistant. Therefore, he may be more willing to take a look at what is happening with him. Vicki says,

> It's my guess that part of his behavior could be childlike: "you can't make me be responsible and predictable like you."

This type of response would also be typical of his personality.

Look to God

As a peer, Kim offers some spiritual encouragement to Christine—and any other women in a similar situation—saying:

> I know what you are feeling because I have been in your shoes. I had to realize that ultimately God is the provider for our family, and He's always watching out for us. God must be your security, no matter what your husband's job situation might be. Read the many Scriptures that teach about God's faithful provision for all our needs (not luxuries!), and let go of the worry over the constant changes and lack of security.

If your marriage is in a comparable circumstance you might want to write some of the verses addressing security on index cards and tape them to your bathroom mirror, the refrigerator, or the dashboard on your car—somewhere you can easily see them throughout the day. Here are a couple of the verses to help you start your study:

> So my counsel is: Don't worry about *things*—food, drink, and clothes. For you already have life and a body—and they are far more important than what to eat and wear. Look at the birds! They don't worry about what to eat—they don't need to sow or reap or store up food—for your heavenly Father feeds them. And you are far more valuable to him than they are. (Matthew 6:25–26 LB)

> All who listen to me shall live in peace and safety, unafraid. (Proverbs 1:33 LB)

Different Times, Different Personalities

In dealing with her husband's job changes, Kim had to realize that times have changed. Even if her husband worked for a company for twenty years, there is no guarantee of security. People get laid off from seemingly secure jobs every day.

Additionally, Steve and Christine's personalities aggravate the situation. As a Perfect Melancholy, security and stability are very important to Christine. She has managed her professional life so that it provides her with the consistency she needs. In her childhood home, her father probably provided for the family, and she entered into her marriage believing that Steve would do the same for her. On the other hand, Steve has a built-in desire for change. He likes a challenge and is generally resilient to setbacks. He has repeatedly picked himself up, dusted himself off, and started over again—facing the world with the confidence typical of a Powerful Choleric with some Popular Sanguine. However, these very strengths have become weaknesses in his relationship with Christine.

When Kim looked at her husband's personality, she had to learn that God created her husband as he is—bold, entrepreneurial spirit and all. She exhorts Christine from her own experience:

The fact that many more people fail at attempting such ventures than succeed is quite beside the point to the bold men we're married to. But that's because our men have a hard time learning from others. They are much more inclined to learn by charting their own course and doing things on their own, including making their own mistakes. Keep in mind that this concept has been ingrained in our men by their fathers and society as a whole. It's called rugged individualism, where legendary men throughout the ages have pulled themselves up by their own bootstraps and against all odds conquered some seemingly impossible feat. Men love the scenario when it is the bottom of the ninth, two outs, nobody on base, and the team needs a miraculous home run to win the big game.

While men like Steve do have that need for change, the wife's inherent need for security must be addressed as well. Chuck suggests that couples in Steve and Christine's predicament discuss the next direction. Together, they need to establish agreeable limits on the ventures to reduce risks, to commit to a specific period of time on a job and not leave despite an opportunity that might appear more interesting, challenging, or profitable than his current position.

Decide Where to Draw the Line

From her experience, Kim questioned our panel of experts,

What about instances of seriously misguided intentions that you are certain will lead to catastrophe? How do you take a stand about an issue with an ambitious husband who doesn't listen very well to what you say?

The key can be in a relational technique called "differentiation." Differentiation means drawing a clear line between yourself and your spouse, and learning to speak up for what you believe in a loving but effective way. The opposite of differentiation is emotional fusion: when you and your spouse are so entwined emotionally that when one of you is having a crisis, the other can't help but be sucked in. It's healthier for individuals to stand on their own two feet so that one or both can remain balanced and bring needed perspective to a situation.

Here's how differentiation has worked for Kim and her husband.

David's foray into day trading followed on the heels of a start-up retail business. There were many reasons why that venture didn't work out the way he wanted it to, and it was disappointing to both of us. Together, these two endeavors ate up about 18 months of David's time and optimism, by the end of which we were both feeling very run down and burned out. When he decided to conclude his day trading experiment, his natural response was to start looking for another entrepreneurial venture to get into. But I really wanted him just to work for an established company and get a regular paycheck coming in! I didn't care if he changed jobs a time or two in searching for the best opportunity, but I was positive I didn't want to watch him start yet another new business.

On a Saturday morning, I sat down with David and spoke up about what I felt I needed in terms of his career direction at this juncture. I said, "Honey, I'm sorry it hasn't worked out for you to build your own company right now. I know that's what you really desire. But I need you to know what effect your path has had on me these past eighteen months. I am tired of the constant challenges and changes. I don't feel that I can handle watching any more business ventures on your part. What I really need is a break from the craziness and uncertainty, and so do you. I'm asking you for a two-year ban on all new business start-up ventures so that we can get back on our feet financially and emotionally. I need for you to get a regular job and stick with it at least two years. I'm not saying I never want you to go into business for yourself again, but for right now I need two years away from that scene."

I didn't get hysterical as I was saying this; I didn't cry; I didn't say "I told you so." I kept under control and made my stand. If

I had gotten upset and cried, or made angry accusations, or gotten irrational—I would have been operating in emotional fusion, not differentiation.

David was rather surprised by my bold stand, but he respected me for it and really, perhaps for the first time, understood where I was coming from. Fortunately, he accepted my request and agreed to the two-year moratorium. David found a job with an established company in the field of advertising where he had experienced success before his entrepreneurial ventures. This new company allows him a great deal of autonomy, and he even gets to work from his home office. So David practically feels self-employed, although he is technically an employee with a biweekly paycheck and benefits. God has given him the best of both worlds and he's never been happier!

Establish Accountability

Assuming couples in this place can discuss their situation as Kim and David did (it may need to be done with a counselor) and reach an agreement, Chuck recommends that men get an accountability partner. The concept of an accountability partner is widely used in the secular world but frequently is missing in the Christian community. In our sample case history, Steve should have another male—his pastor, Bible study leader, a counselor, or a solid Christian friend—who will meet with him periodically to hold him to the agreement he has made with his wife. This takes her out of the dangerous position of being the bad cop. It also gives him someone he respects on whom he can vent his frustrations without causing undue stress to his wife.

Accept Differences, Forge Ahead

Christine has accepted that Steve is different. She now needs to give him some credit for his optimism and for the fact that he keeps trying and has not given up in despair. A woman in Christine's place needs to realize that her husband will probably never have the long-term security she observed in her childhood home—society is no longer structured that way and, in the presenting problem's example, Steve was never wired that way.

If you can make these changes in your attitudes and behaviors and if he is willing to make a short-term commitment that will allow you to build up some savings, you will have a better sense of security and will be more accepting of future transitions. Kim says,

> I wish I had realized sooner about keeping my eyes on God for my family's security. I wish I would have known earlier about God's design for men like my husband, as well as society's influence on their behavior. But I am so thankful that these lessons have only taken the first fifteen years of our marriage! I believe we will have at least that many and more of harmony between us—no matter what direction David's career takes.

Depression

Beware and Seek Counsel if Necessary

While Steve has remained optimistic overall, which is typical of his personality, Christine is concerned for the depression he faces after a failure. The Powerful Choleric is typically fairly stable emotionally, but the Popular Sanguine is known for emotional ups and downs—very up when things are going well and covered with a huge black cloud when things are not. Though depression like Steve's is probably not life threatening, it is wearing and is detrimental to the marriage. It needs some attention.

Margie faced a situation similar to Christine's in her marriage. From her experience, she offers the following peer insight:

> My husband had several disappointments in the corporate world and stepped into an entrepreneurial opportunity. It failed and we lost a huge investment as well as our retirement monies. It began a downward spiral of depression.

When Margie's husband was able to find another job, it required that he be away from home and the family during the week. This plus the effects of his depression and recession from reality "cannot be repaired," Margie reports:

> Looking in, I could see the obvious signs of depression years ago. But I could not get him to acknowledge it, let alone do anything about it. He simply moved farther away, both in his work and emotions. Unfortunately, I did not understand the repercussions. Had I sought help, I believe we would have saved everyone in our family tremendous problems, pain, grief, and even perhaps the impending divorce. The problem just kept building until the dam burst!

With this background, Margie encourages Christine and Steve to get professional counseling to look at the reasons for his frequent job changes.

Demand it if necessary. He is at risk and so is your future security.

Adjust and Support

As Christine is able to adjust her attitudes and behaviors, she will be able to be more supportive of Steve. Her acceptance is apt to remove some of the pressure from Steve, thereby lessening his potential for depression when things do not work out. When Christine's security comes from Christ, she will have peace. While she hopes Steve's efforts will pay off and that he does find the right position for his skills and personality, she can love and respect him for his many other qualities—the ones that attracted her to him in the first place.

Kim and David worked to focus on those good qualities in their relationship. She told me,

> Even throughout the toughest times in David's career, we have worked to find areas of mutual enjoyment in our lives. We love to travel together. Sometimes we could afford only a brief weekend getaway, but we've treasured those times. We also love to take walks on the beach. It's good for our bodies and souls. We

like eating out and going to movies, when finances allow. We both love trivia, so we'll quiz each other out of books or articles we've read. The point is not to lose sight of what is good and positive in your marriage, no matter what the challenges are.

After all, this is what the modern marriage is about. It is different from what many of us saw in our parents' marriage—yet the core needs of love, trust, and respect remain. Trust and respect are not based on a paycheck, dollars, or business. While society places a high value on these monetary indicators, real love, a real relationship, rises above that—that is love extravagant!

The Interactions

For couples in a similar situation to Steve and Christine, Chuck would assign the following "homework" assignment:

1. Together, agree upon a Christian friend to whom the husband will be accountable. He should not make any job changes without the go-ahead of the accountability partner. This frees the wife from having to be the cop, while restraining him from job or entrepreneurial changes.
2. The wife must make a commitment to be an emotional support and encouragement to the husband. Building his self-esteem may contribute to his job success. She might bring him lunch, send him cards or flowers, or celebrate with his favorite meal when he meets certain milestones—these might be major sales or months on the job.
3. The couple should discuss, agree upon, and write out short- and long-term joint goals. The husband's job/career plans can then be measured against the goals.
4. Diagram a career map. This map may be words and/or pictures or even cartoons—the first things that come to mind—that illustrate his various jobs and the elements that he especially liked and/or disliked. Additionally, add how he felt during that job. The jobs may indicate an up-and-down pattern to his moods.

Discovering what jobs—or elements of certain jobs—helped or hurt his depression will help with future job decisions. This is important, as fun is a vital aspect for his personality type and a job where there is some fun, will help with his satisfaction. Next, search for the commonalities within the strengths and weaknesses of each position. This will help him learn what to avoid for the future and, more importantly, what he is looking for in a job—benefits like fun, respect, and rewards.

Nine

Twenty-four/Seven Togetherness

Doing Business Together, Separating Business and Personal Life

The Issue

Wes and Tina own a retail business and have worked together for the past thirteen years. Over the years they have encountered a variety of challenges and because their personalities are very different, usually approach them differently. The fact that Tina is a Christian and Wes is not affects how they view the importance of the business in their life and how it affects their lives overall. As a man, Wes's sense of identity and worth revolves around the success or failure of the business much more than Tina's does.

Through many discussions and arguments over the years, they have learned how to work pretty well together. Wes and Tina recognize their different strengths and weaknesses that bring balance to the relationship. They have also realized that there can be only one "boss" with ultimate responsibility for decision making. Decisions are discussed regarding policies or employees, for example, but Wes has the ultimate final say. Basically they get along great, love each other, usually like each other, and have a wonderful time when they are away. They enjoy the business most of the time.

Their biggest challenge has been—and continues to be—how to separate their business life from their personal life. They live in a small town and everywhere they go they see the same people who shop in their store. They are together every day, and everything that happens at work goes home with them and affects the mood there. Wes and Tina have no children on whom to focus their attention; there is nothing new to share about the day because each already knows exactly what went on.

If they have a disagreement about how to handle a problem at work, they can't help but take it personally, even though they know they shouldn't. Then it affects their relationship as husband and wife.

The Insights

Many marriages need to work at spending time together. For the couple in business or ministry together, one of the challenges is spending time apart! The business can easily become all-consuming. The same can be true for couples who are together in ministry. For most couples who work together, the problems seem to boil down to two specific areas: business and personal.

Doing Business Together

Wes and Tina's story indicates that through "disagreements and arguments" they have already discovered a problem area common to many couples in business together: different strengths and weaknesses.

Divide and Conquer

Whenever I speak on marriage and how Chuck and I are opposites, heads nod in agreement to the idea that we usually marry someone whose personality is opposite from our own. Because this is often a source of conflict, people question God's wisdom in this natural attraction. I believe that when God said the two should become one

(Gen. 2:24) He had the opposite personalities in mind. Because Chuck and I have very different strengths and weaknesses, we balance out and stabilize one another. Where I am weak, he is strong, and where he is less gifted, I am more skilled. Together we bring a full complement of skills to the table. When we can understand this, we can use it to our advantage.

When a husband and wife run a business together, these differences can be a terrific asset or they can be a terrible detriment. It's great that, between the two, virtually all skills needed to run the business can be found. The key is to allow each individual to use his or her areas of giftedness.

In Bob and Sherrie's situation, they found that once they understood their personalities, they worked together much better in their family farm business:

> We pay a lot of attention to our personality traits. This helps immensely! Understanding why the other ticks the way they do allows us to delegate certain aspects of our life apart from the farm. For instance, Bob took on the budget and set up a system that keeps us on the same page without cumbersome and repeated arguments. I am responsible to keep a "honey-do" list running so that in his spare time he can get to the home repairs. He keeps the vehicles fueled and serviced; I keep up the laundry.

The difficulties arise when both spouses have a large percentage of Powerful Choleric or when the personality type runs contrary to expected gender-specific roles.

When husband and wife have the Powerful Choleric Personality in common—which is often the case when a couple is in business together—they tend to battle for control. This was the case for Tony and Amanda. They owned a photo lab for several years. The front of the shop was a retail store where they sold cameras and related items and took in the film to process. The back contained the lab and all the equipment to process the film. Offering peer insight, Amanda shares what they did to deal with this problem:

We basically split the business in two parts. Tony functioned as the technician, in charge of everything in the lab, and I was the up-front person, in charge of everything in the store. This fit our personalities perfectly. I am Popular Sanguine and Powerful Choleric, and he is Perfect Melancholy and Powerful Choleric. He was the boss behind the door and I was the boss in front of the door. Although we made decisions together, we still had our own domains to manage. This kept us from running over each other, both mentally and physically! It worked very well and we never had problems of power—amazing for two people heavy with Powerful Choleric personality!

Chuck and I have this same personality blend in our marriage. We are not in business together day in and day out, but we have been working on this book together and plan to work on others. While both of us are naturally "take charge" people, we have had to divide up duties. We agreed before we ever started who would do what, and we have honored our plans. Since I am the writer and he is the therapist, we agreed that I would be the one to actually write the book. His fingers have never touched the keyboard, but we reviewed the scenarios, discussed ideas, and worked on it together. I have worked on the areas of my strength and he on his.

If one spouse is more naturally gifted in a specific area, it would be foolish to give the other authority over that domain. My parents were in ministry together for years and shared this potentially conflicting personality combination in marriage—both of them having a large portion of Powerful Choleric. They, too, divided the duties. My mother as the gifted professional speaker was in charge of the stage, the "up front," and my father with a background in business was in charge of everything behind the scenes. Occasionally they shared the platform, but since that is my mother's expertise, she was in charge of what goes on there. When they discussed business or financial dealings, that was my father's turf.

This division of labor works well when two Powerful Cholerics are involved in business together—whether or not they are married. But it is essential when you are married to your business partner. You can't fire him or her, and you have to go home and sleep together. As Wes and Tina's scenario points out, while you try not to take it personally, you do take the disagreements home with you. So it is best to set things up in such a way that conflicts are minimized.

Allocate Authority

Another way to minimize conflicts is to agree on alternate days to be the decision maker at work. Chuck says,

> Accepting authority and exerting authority are opposite sides of the same coin. One must be able to be a good private to be a good general. By agreeing to trade off who makes the decisions, you avoid a "one up, one down relationship" which is counter to the scriptural concept of mutual submission.

There are times when stalemates will happen, no matter what. Kurt and Stephanie share some of the same concerns expressed by Wes and Tina. They each have their own business, and both businesses are run out of their home. Stephanie says,

> When we can't arrive at a mutually agreeable solution or reach a compromise, we often wait and don't make a decision at all. This allows us both time to reevaluate the situation. Many times things do not need to be decided right away. I believe that God has given us a hierarchy to follow, and Kurt and I have established that his decisions are the final ones. This only works if the other spouse lives by these terms and does not pout or try to sway the other into changing his or her mind. Two bosses never work.

While some women may have trouble with Stephanie's approach, someone has to have fifty-one percent of the vote. Scripturally, that is to be the man. First Corinthians 11:3 says,

> But there is one thing I want you to know: A man is responsible

to Christ, a woman is responsible to her husband, and Christ is responsible to God. (NLT)

Addressing that verse, the *Life Application Bible* study notes say,

> Submission is a key element in the smooth functioning of any business, government, or family. God ordained submission in certain relationships to prevent chaos. It is essential to understand that submission is not surrender, withdrawal, or apathy. It does not mean inferiority, because God created all people in his image and because all have equal value. Submission is mutual commitment and cooperation.

Gender Roles

Opposite personalities married to one another and in business together can also be a problem when the personality types are contrary to traditional gender roles, as is the case with my sister, Lauren, and her husband, Randy. She is naturally gifted in business, has a head for numbers, and is a take charge kind of person. Randy, a historian, is gifted in his field and highly respected for his expertise, honesty, and integrity in an industry fraught with deception. He and his partner own a seventy-year-old business that deals with stamps, coins, precious metals, and other collectibles and antiquities.

Lauren was brought into the business because she had skills that would be an asset to the organization and would free Randy to do what he does best. Being a Powerful Choleric, she is a doer and a natural problem solver. She brought the business from no computers, everything done by hand, "but we've always done it this way," to computerization, Web site development, and Internet trading—but not without resistance. As the Peaceful Phlegmatic who doesn't like change, Randy did not always see the need for the advancements Lauren was suggesting.

In looking back over the last twenty-plus years in business together, Lauren sees that the key to their successful business relationship has been to respect each other and their differences, and be grateful for strengths and gifts they each have. As a Powerful Choleric, it could be easy for her to overlook Randy's less up-front skills and casual approach. As a Peaceful Phlegmatic, Randy could easily resent her obvious skills and quick decisions. Over the years they have learned to work together by appreciating each other's abilities and realizing that their talents lie in very different areas—both of which are needed in the business. Since Lauren holds the aptitude for the more typically male tasks, it would be foolish for Randy to do them. While he is capable of fulfilling these duties, they are not his. Since he does not enjoy the tasks, he puts them off. Most importantly, when Lauren works where she is most effective, Randy can work where he is at his best. Together they bring a full complement of skills to the table.

However, typical male/female expectations created some initial stress for them. It appeared that Lauren was trying to take over. Lauren viewed that she was just fixing the problems and making things better. They had to discuss what areas were Lauren's and what were Randy's.

Additionally, they had to learn what Randy wanted Lauren's input on, and what he did not. Part of Randy's inherent personality is an eye for the negative. He would be thinking out loud about a problem that had been a part of the business for years. Hearing him talk about the problem, Lauren's natural problem-solving ability kicked in and she began to offer solutions. He resisted her advice, and she was frustrated when her suggestions were not implemented and the same issues were rehashed again at a later date. They have worked to define what they do or do not want. When Randy complains, Lauren now asks, "Do you want a solution for this?" Or, Randy may say at the beginning of a conversation, "I just want to talk, I am not looking for answers or opinions." Lauren then knows to take off her business partner hat and put on her caring wife demeanor. This has made a big difference in their working relationship.

From their experience, Lauren and Randy offer these tips to all couples who work together and have differing personalities:

- Respect the difference you each have.
- Be grateful for the gifts and skills your partner has that are different from yours.
- Don't resent your partner when he or she does not view things

the way you do. It is not a negative that he or she doesn't have the same gifts you have.

Understanding each other's personality—strengths and weaknesses—and defining who is in charge of what—regardless of gender—are two things that can make business better for couples who work together.

Separating Business and Personal Life

The other problem that seems to be shared by all couples in business together is trying have a personal life apart from the business. Everyone who responded to Wes and Tina's situation agreed that separating the business life from personal life is one of the biggest challenges.

Buffer for Balance

To find that balance, Chuck suggests that couples dealing with a dilemma like Wes and Tina's, develop some sort of a ritual or buffer between work and home life that will allow them to take off the "work" hat and shed the "work" clothing.

> Go to a gym, go jogging, walk the dog, do some relaxation exercises, study the Bible—anything that will pair a physical action with the cognitive process of mentally changing hats. The goal is to stop thinking about work and start thinking about the home life. We are all made up of different "selves" or "personas." There may be a professional self, a personal self, a husband or wife, a parent, and so on. Much of the difficulty people experience in communication is rooted in confusing our roles and the parameters that go with them. When the military officer comes home and lines the family up for inspection, trouble follows. A change of thinking is needed. However, it is hard to stop a thought process or drop a persona that has been used successfully all day. It is easier to change what we're doing than to change our behavior. This is why creating an actual buffer between home and work is important.

Create Zones

Next, Chuck advises that they create a work-free time or "zone." They might agree that from 6:30 P.M. to 7:00 A.M. is personal time and that work will not be discussed in any way during those hours. The work-free zone might mean that you agree not to discuss work at the dinner table or in the bedroom. Those zones would be free from work. Chuck says,

> Do the best you can. Turn off the cell phone and forward the home phone to voice mail or just let it ring. Couples could institute a "work-free game." Each time someone talks about work during the agreed upon work-free time, they would chip twenty-five cents into a date fund.

Life Outside of Work

These ideas will help separate the home and business worlds. Additionally, couples who work together need to develop a life outside of work, both individually and together. Addressing that need for balance, Michelle Holman, MA, LPC, observed that our case history couple, Wes and Tina, do not seem to have anything going on in their life that does not revolve around work. She offers all wives in Tina's situation the following advice:

> I would encourage her to utilize a small group of church friends to give her an alternate place to vent and have fun. Our world can grow so large that it strains the relationships in the home, but its growing too small will have the same effect. Having a "lunch buddy" whom she meets with weekly, someone separate from her work and married life, might be another way to develop additional quality relationships.

Carey and his wife are also in business together. He says,

> We, too, live in a small town. We are very visible, so we feel like we are never away from our jobs. A couple of things that

have helped us might be beneficial to others in this situation as well. First, we spend as much time apart as we can—pursuing separate interests—so that we have something to talk about. I try to have "guy nights" where I have some friends over and we watch sci-fi movies and eat pizza. My wife takes our son to a friend's house or goes to a scrapbooking party or goes shopping with a friend.

Chuck applauds the efforts that Carey and his wife have made to develop individual interests. He says,

> Couples that work and live together can have a little too much togetherness. They can become emotionally enmeshed. Somewhere between detached and enmeshed is a healthy balance that will be different for each couple. Healthy couples have intimacy, yet make allowances for distance.

So couples who work together, as Wes and Tina do, are encouraged to develop individual interests and friendships to give them some time apart, to help them grow and develop conversation that does not revolve around the business.

Creative Time Together

In addition to the individual things they can do, couples should also put some effort and creativity into doing things together that are totally different from their daily lives. Chapter 5, "Lack of Time Together," offers several suggestions for creative time together which may be helpful to Wes and Tina and all couples in business together. Couples agree that creativity is one key that has helped keep their relationship fresh and interesting.

Continuing his suggestions based on what he and his wife have done to keep their relationship fresh and interesting, Carey offers this peer insight:

> We try to schedule one date night a month where we get out of

our small town and do something out of the ordinary. It doesn't have to be expensive, but it does have to be creative. We have gone to a museum on a Friday night where they have chamber music and appetizers that you can enjoy for just the admission price. We have also gone rollerblading, and attended softball games and pigged out on junk food, and we've tried new restaurants in our area. Every six months or so we try to arrange for childcare and get out of town for a romantic weekend. It takes creativity and work, but you can have separate hobbies and find things to talk about, even when you work together.

Bob and Sherrie found that date nights worked well for them too. However, they had to set some ground rules. Sherrie says,

> Bob and I scheduled "date nights," which we kept whether or not we wanted to. The only criterion was that we not discuss the farm in any way! At first it was awkward; we found we had little to talk about. We got one of those marriage builder books that set up discussion topics. Again it was awkward and felt mechanical, but we needed a jump-start. As time went on, we would jot down things we wanted to share with one another on our date.

For those of you in business or ministry together, like Wes and Tina, loving each other with extravagance may mean adjusting your expectations of your professional selves based on personality and skills rather than gender roles. It may mean being willing to divide responsibilities or trade off days of being the "boss." Make time for yourselves and make time to keep fun in the marriage. In all cases, the business must be secondary to the marriage. Your marriage must be your priority. Follow the suggestions found here and you'll find it pays big dividends!

The Interactions

For couples in a similar situation to Wes and Tina, Chuck would assign the following "homework" assignment:

1. Develop a buffer between work and home. The husband and wife should each design and implement a daily after-work "buffer." This may be as simple as leaving a hat in the car or the gold jacket in the office—if that works. Most people need a more complex ritual to be successful with this. Physical activity with repetitive motion like watching one foot go in front of the other while running or watching the front wheel go around on a bicycle is good. Change into your exercise clothes on the way out of the business. Think about the breath going in and out and pair this with self-talk saying, "I am not at work anymore. I will not think about work again until the alarm goes off tomorrow." Develop a plan for walking in the front door of your home: "First thing I am going to do is hug my wife; then I am going to hug the kids." Be creative. Do what you have to do.
2. Create a work-free time or zone. Schedule and implement a time or place when work will not be discussed in any way. This could be from 6:30–8:30 each evening or while in the dining room or bedroom. Bring your home under your own control. It may also be necessary to designate a scheduled time to "vent" about work. Learn how to commiserate and say "poor baby." Avoid projecting anger about someone else onto your spouse. Your spouse is the last person you want to get mad at. Get the frustration out so once you get home, you can focus on the here and now.
3. Design a "work-free zone" game. Create and implement a fun game that tracks the violations of the "work-free zone." Write out the rules on a poster. This will help make the unconscious tendency to lapse back into the work role conscious and under our control. The couple might decide to put twenty-five cents into a piggy bank for each violation. There could be a whistle blown to signal a foul. The offender might agree to give the other spouse a five-minute back rub. Be creative. The crazy stuff will stay in your memory.
4. Develop something all your own. Each spouse should identify and develop an activity that is solely his or her own. Time should be set aside, guilt-free, to invest in this aspect of yourself. It is also important to budget money for these activities. Additionally, each

spouse should select a personal space in the home that is just his or hers. This could be a corner for a piano or a sewing machine, or room in the garage for a roll-about toolbox. Trust and respect in a marriage require the opportunity for privacy and security. This is especially important for the Perfect Melancholies.

PART 3
FINANCIAL ISSUES

Ten

Merging Finances

Prenuptial Agreements, Creating Connectedness

The Issue

Kathy and Mark are newly married. She is thirty-nine and he is forty-four. It is a second marriage for both of them. They are both strong financially. Mark has built a successful business and Kathy is part-owner of her father's real estate business and holdings—which has supported her and her daughter for the last fifteen years. However, Kathy is finding it difficult to orchestrate finances with Mark. In an attempt to honor her father and help him to not feel threatened, Mark and Kathy agreed to sign a prenuptial agreement, keeping their finances separate.

They contribute equally to a joint account that pays their household expenses, but they are finding it difficult to feel connected in their marriage. There is no real sense of working together for their future or for that of their four children (three are his and one is hers). Mark struggles with the fact that he is not truly the provider for the family. They are trying to find a middle ground to avoid having to separate totally from her father's business in order to have peace. The agreement seemed like a good idea and smart in a business sense in the beginning, but now it makes their marriage feel like a business arrangement instead of a "one flesh" union.

The Insights

This particular dilemma presents two specific issues common to many modern marriages. One is the merging of two financial houses and styles of money management—often based in a prenuptial agreement—and the other is how to develop a sense of connectedness in the new family. As you will see, other couples in similar circumstances, as well as the contributing therapists, recognize these as two different, possibly unrelated, situations. Depending on the situation at your house, one part may apply more to you than the other.

Prenuptial Agreements

In an Ozzie-and-Harriet world, prenuptial agreements were not an issue. Couples usually married young before either had an opportunity to acquire any assets. They started in a small apartment with nothing but their wedding presents and some borrowed furniture. Together they built what became their net worth. She raised the children and managed their home responsibly while offering him the emotional support he needed to function at his best as he earned the family's income. They had no need for a prenuptial agreement. Chuck's grandparents "Ma and Pa" were married seventy-five years. Over the years, Pa told his grandchildren the story of their wedding day. As they left the marriage ceremony Pa realized that he had one coin in his pocket. He took it out and tossed it over his left shoulder so he and Ma could start out "even."

Financial History

Today, many marriages face situations similar to that of Kathy and Mark. When one or both spouses is established financially, has their own investments, and is used to being in control of their own monetary destiny, it is very difficult to let go completely and offer their spouse everything they have worked so hard to achieve. This is especially true when either or both the husband and wife have a history with a former spouse where money was either spent foolishly or used as a tool for control.

Sherrie's history with her former husband colored her new marriage.

> From experience, I can say that second marriages are prone to over-sensitivity. The couple doesn't start from ground zero when it comes to building a life together. We often enter the marriage with wounds and sensitivities—some have been healed, others remain hidden. Though our financial situation was composed of different elements than Kathy and Mark, my husband and I were both uptight in the money arena. I chose to give up my career in the city to become a farmer's wife and a stay-at-home mom. In addition to feeling like a "slacker" for not contributing to the household budget, I felt powerless and vulnerable. I worried about being abandoned again.

The world's resolution for this modern marriage problem is the prenuptial agreement. However, there is no scriptural foundation for this concept, and it is adverse to the biblical concept of "leave and cleave."

An Issue of Trust

Chuck has found that whatever the situation, a prenuptial agreement is "pure poison." He would never suggest a prenuptial agreement in premarital counseling. Gaylen Larson, PhD, agrees:

> The problem with a prenuptial agreement is that it says "I don't trust you or this relationship to last." As trust is a core basis of any marriage, a prenuptial agreement is just the opposite of what is needed.

Throw Out or Phase Out

But since Kathy and Mark already have one, Chuck suggests that couples with a prenuptial agreement develop a plan to begin to phase out the agreement. Think about how long you would have to be married to be able to trust each other. For example, he asks, "If you are married twenty years, would you still need a prenuptial agreement?" Most couples he has counseled scoff at the thought of needing such an agreement after twenty years. "What about ten? What about five?" he asks. Discuss at what point the prenuptial agreement would be a moot issue and plan to phase it out accordingly.

Maxine Marsolini, author of *Blended Families*, adds,

> Trust between husband and wife needs to develop throughout the marriage and the stepfamily before the agreement should be done away with entirely. After reading the issues between Mark and Kathy, I sense them blaming the prenuptial agreement for their inability to set goals for their blended family. Realize it is always possible to set family financial goals. There is money going into the joint account. The question is, are you willing to work together in the best interest of every family member?

As a peer advisor, Reanna found that trust was a key issue in her marriage to Tim. Both had been married before. When they had a prenuptial agreement drawn up, Reanna had convinced herself that it was really to protect Tim from her student loan problems with the potential threat of having her bank account attached. But, she says,

> As time has gone by, I have realized that this is really about me wanting to retain my independence, not trusting Tim with finances, and not wanting to answer to anyone about how I spent my money.

Now that Reanna and Tim have been married for seven years, Reanna can see the error of her ways and they are taking steps to correct their situation. She continues,

> Tim has never wanted to do things this way. I always felt like I needed to control "my money." Since I bring in more than he does, I have felt that I have a right. Now, I can see that we do not have a complete union. We split up bills like roommates. God has been speaking to my heart about our separateness in finan-

cial affairs. It has been the source of nearly all our arguments. I have been in bondage to money as a result. I have lifted this up in prayer—wanting to stop depending on myself for financial security. This is not something that can be worked out logically as much as spiritually. I could have handed these things over to Tim from the beginning, but then I would have been resentful and still trying to control things. God has been doing a work in me from the inside out.

From her personal experience, Reanna encourages couples facing the prenuptial problem as Kathy and Mark are, to do some soul searching and come to a place of trust.

This is not something that can be worked out logically. If we go with logic alone, a prenuptial agreement might sound like a good idea. I remember my attorney's advice before I got married. Since I owned my own business and some real estate, he suggested that Chuck and I have a prenuptial agreement. When I listened to his side, it sounded logical. I approached Chuck about it. Chuck's reaction was that a prenuptial agreement was like planning to fail and I agreed. We did not draw one up.

While a prenuptial agreement makes sense in the ways of the world, it gets down to the question, what are you really committed to? The money or the marriage? Part of being married is dying to self—loving extravagantly.

Stephanie and Kurt also had a prenuptial agreement when they got married. Stephanie reports,

> It was a second marriage for both of us. It wasn't until we started attending some marriage classes that we realized this agreement was totally against God's plan for marriages. True "one flesh" marriage includes the income. Kurt and I each own our own businesses. We don't always agree on policies and procedures, but we are in agreement that all our income is ours—not his or mine. We have learned to totally depend on the Lord for our finances. Ultimately, all of our blessings, income, and material gain are His and come from Him. We would urge all

couples to do as we did. We burned our agreement at a group meeting—made it public. It was a real testimony. Christians need to learn to stand up for what God has instituted and not compromise.

If you have a prenuptial agreement, whether official and legal, or simply verbally agreed on, look at the cause of its existence. Are there trust and/or control issues present? Is your relationship now at a place where you can begin to phase it out or tear it up as Stephanie and Kurt did? Whichever direction you determine is right for the equilibrium of your situation, if you have a prenuptial agreement in place, get some specific guidance before abandoning it so you do not create legal trouble for yourself.

Parental Involvement

While Chuck and I did not have a prenuptial agreement, we did face some of the same problems Kathy and Mark are facing. I owned my own business when we got married. Trends changed, and about seven years into our marriage, I had to close my business and find another source of income. For several years I struggled to earn a living from a variety of sources. What seemed to be the best fit evolved from the work I had been doing with my parents. Eventually, I joined them in their business and became a vital part of their activities—earning more than I had ever made before or since. This was my best period of income, but it was the worst time for my marriage.

I was constantly torn between my parents and honoring them and cleaving to my husband. We reached a crisis point where I had to be willing to walk away from the security the family business provided and place my husband and my marriage first. The end result was that I did not have to find an entirely new career or leave the family business, but I had to be willing to do so. Eventually, we found a plan that worked for everyone involved. I now own a portion of what was once my parents' business—which I run as I see fit. My mother still owns the part of the business that was her passion from the start. We operate cooperatively, but independently. From my experience, I would encourage anyone in Kathy's position to look at ways that they might be able to restructure any professional relationship with parents if there is a potential crisis in the marriage.

From his experience as a therapist, Chuck discourages adults working for their parents. It can be successful, but working for one's parents makes the process of reaching peerhood with your parents very difficult. Failing to reach peerhood with parents can result in husband and wife being on unequal footing—with one "parenting" the other.

Creating Connectedness

In the presenting problem, Kathy and Mark also have a need for a sense of working together in their marriage. This is not strictly a financial issue but more one of personal development. Many couples face this problem even when there are no monetary issues. Michelle Holman, LPC, would work with couples like Kathy and Mark to help them understand that intimacy involves more than sharing business goals. She says,

> Intimacy comes from being an authentic individual who shares with someone else one's true self and is willing to risk the vulnerability that comes with this. If Kathy and Mark are simply wanting to be more connected in their finances, the joint household account's purposes could be enlarged to include contributing to family goals such as children's education, vacations, and special activities.

Kathy states that Mark does not feel as if he is truly the provider for the family. Again, money is not the only way to provide for one's family. Mark could focus on providing spiritual leadership, being a good example for their children, and offering a shoulder to cry on when needed. All of these are much needed aspects of providing for his family. Michelle Holman says,

> If Mark is struggling with the idea that he is not truly being the provider for the family, where did he learn that he "should" be?

Has he been taught tradition or Scripture? Biblically, being the head of a home doesn't mean that he must be the sole source of income. The Proverbs 31 woman contributed to her household.

Additionally, in a situation like the case history, Kathy should be grateful that her husband wants to be the provider in an age when many men shirk their responsibilities.

Joint Goals

To bring the financial and connectedness concerns together, Kathy and Mark need to work cooperatively on some joint goals. This can be done even if their prenuptial agreement remains in place or while they are working to phase it out. Jane's situation is similar, although she does not think that she and her husband ever felt less than "one flesh." Their marriage is the second for both. They maintain separate accounts and have a joint account for household expenses. Jane has no children and her husband has one son. From her experience, Jane offers the following peer insight:

> Sit down together and talk about the plans for the future. If necessary, do this with a counselor, but you may be able to do this yourselves. Establish goals as a couple. It might be helpful for each spouse to make a wish list and then bring the lists together. These goals need not be financial only, but could include things like weekly Bible study together, one spouse cleaning the bathroom weekly, or a regular date night. Many couples need to work on their homes and yards. New vehicles, vacations, and retirement must be planned for. Charitable giving should also be discussed. Once the lists have been made, prioritize; deciding what to tackle first and developing a timeline. In this way, the couple feels that they are working together to build a home and marriage.

Working together to build a home and a marriage is what Marge and Jesse found they needed to do. Their situation was similar to Kathy and Mark's. Marge made quite a bit more money than Jesse and was reluctant to give him access to all her earnings and holdings. Her first marriage had been a financial fiasco, and she was still recovering from the damage her ex-husband had caused. One of the many things they did was to take a large portion of their individual earnings and use them for joint investments. They also decided to sell the home where they were living. It had been Jesse's home before they got married and remained in his name only. They bought a new home to start together and it carries both of their names on the mortgage.

Along the same lines, Melanie Wilson, PhD, suggests that couples seeking financial connectedness get involved in a financial project together. She says,

> Perhaps it is something their children could even help with. For example the family could decide that they have a goal of buying a vacation home. They could research together where to purchase it, how much it would cost, etc. Then they could budget and invest money toward that goal. Perhaps they could research stocks or mutual funds that would help them reach the goal.

With these cooperative goals, several suggested that Kathy's income contribute more heavily toward vacations, retirement, and college funds while Mark's money could go into providing household finances. Robin Jackson, a financial software developer, suggested this solution:

> Create a college savings plan for each of the four children. Working together doesn't have to mean only one account from which all monies are drawn. A great example of this is Fidelity Investment's Unique College Investing Plan. While only one person can be the account owner with one beneficiary (the child), both spouses can contribute to the fund and watch it grow as a family. Letting the children know about their investment account and going online to check its growth can be a very good way to teach them about planning ahead, delaying gratification, and feeling secure.

From "He" and "She" to "We"

Robin also suggested another option, a revocable living trust that would make a "we" out of the "he" and "she." The trust would be a legal entity that would hold the assets they want to share. Often a trust can be a way to preserve assets from a previous marriage for the children. In cases where the children's father has died and whose life insurance was purchased with the goal of providing for the children's schooling, these monies need to be set aside so they are there when the kids are ready for college. A trust can do this without threatening the marriage commitment.

Melanie Wilson also recommends that they involve a third party in their finances, and Chuck agrees. Having a third party, such as a financial professional, involved removes either spouse from the control or "cop" position and provides for more cooperative decision making while removing the ability to blame each other for financial mistakes they may make in the future.

Chapter 8, "Career Chaos," and chapter 9, "Twenty-four/Seven Togetherness" are related and will offer additional insight in the area of money management for those struggling with this issue.

Different couples have found solutions that work for their situations—they have written their own script for success. That is what the concept of equilibrium is all about. Whatever direction you decide to go, pray and ask for guidance. Prayer is no place for nonsense. It is a holy place; a place where the innermost being of a person is revealed; a place where two people can share their minds and souls and find a life together.

The Interactions

For couples in a similar situation to Kathy and Mark, Chuck would assign the following "homework" assignment:

1. Each spouse should describe in detail the signs, behaviors, actions, and milestones that would indicate that your husband/wife could be fully trusted.

2. Together, set common goals for the marriage and family. Design signposts that mark progress, indicating how you will know when things are getting better.
3. For those with a prenuptial agreement, work together to design a phase-out schedule for the prenuptial agreement. This could be a timeline in cartoon format with signposts drawn on banner paper. (You can also include The Interaction steps one through three on the timeline.)
4. Each spouse should independently explore and describe fears surrounding giving up autonomy and control. Then brainstorm any other blocks to progress.

Eleven

Who Pays? Who Plays?

Control, Shared Activities

The Issue

Bruce and Janna are in their early twenties and have been married a few years. It is a first marriage for both. Bruce is a Popular Sanguine with some of the easy-going, likeable nature of the Peaceful Phlegmatic. He is in the military. Janna is almost fifty-fifty Perfect Melancholy and Powerful Choleric. She is in retail management and is going to school. When Bruce is not off on a long trip or out to sea, his work hours are very set, as is his income. Being in retail, Janna's hours are often long and can vary greatly, especially during the holidays. Add school to her schedule and she is often away from home much of the time that Bruce is off. As she has been promoted, and promoted again, her income has taken a big leap.

Bruce is due to get out of the service soon. At that time, they hope to move and both go to college full-time. Janna is the stronger personality and the more financially responsible. Bruce is more laid back, a little less mature, and more interested in having a good time. While Janna is working or going to school, Bruce spends time with "the boys" and buys "toys" to entertain himself. Janna is frustrated with him because she is trying to put money away for their college education. He feels that since she is gone, and they do have the money, he has a right to spend it.

The Insights

Bruce and Janna have two key problems that are presented in their situation. Janna makes more money and is the stronger personality. This combination can very easily put her into a position of feeling like the parent—which is unhealthy from either spouse's perspective. Bruce can easily feel controlled by Janna and resent her behaviors, while Janna resents what she perceives as his childlike behavior. We'll call this issue "control." Additionally, their lives already seem to be going separate ways with her focusing on school and work and him spending time in fun activities with his friends. They will need to find time to spend together doing things they both enjoy—"activities."

Control

In reading this chapter's presenting problem, peer advisor Anne felt her stomach turn with remembrance over Bruce and Janna's situation as she said, "I can definitely identify with this." While Anne and her husband's situation is the reverse of Bruce and Janna, they had many of the same problems. In their household Anne is the spender and her husband is the saver, the money conscious person in the relationship. Anne reflects,

> Since the day we were married we have always given each other an allowance. While he thought this was great, I felt like a controlled child. I often resented feeling like Daddy was giving me my weekly allowance for doing my chores.

The control issue is a main concern for Bruce and Janna, especially as Janna, the woman, has the stronger personality. If she does what comes naturally to her—earning money and saving responsibly, while pushing Bruce to do the same—he is likely to feel like a controlled child, the way Anne did. Only for Bruce and Janna's situation the problem tends to be magnified since the female is the more "adult." Most of us were raised expecting that the male would be responsible, while society is often more forgiving of the woman who is thought of as "flighty."

As the Popular Sanguine, Anne says,

> I live for the moment, the fun of it. My husband, being a Perfect Melancholy, couldn't conceive just stopping at Starbucks for a cup of coffee when he could brew a whole pot of it at home for less than half the cost. I, on the other hand, love spontaneity and couldn't understand his boring control. I like to enjoy life. My husband is proud of his accomplishments and the growth of his bank account. After all, in his eyes, his worth depends on it.

Give and Take

Anne and her husband separated after eleven years of marriage. During their three-year separation, they started seeing a marriage counselor. In counseling, they learned that they each needed to give a little and trust each other more. Anne learned,

> I needed to understand where he was coming from. I needed to work harder at saving some money and not just living for today. Also, I needed to help him realize his worth was not in how much he could save. He needed to realize that if he let me breathe, assist with the money decisions, and relax, I would learn to be more responsible.

If couples who are in a situation like Bruce and Janna do not learn some give and take, as Anne and her husband did, they are apt to find themselves separated as well. Georgia Shaffer, Pennsylvania licensed psychologist agrees. She sees that each will "need to do a little 'dying to self' to make it past the rough spots."

From her experience, Anne encourages Janna—and others in a similar place—to learn to compromise:

After all, you are a team. Work together like one. Above all, ask God for guidance and help. Without Him we can do nothing. (John 15:5)

Chuck and I have a similar situation to the problem presented in this chapter. I am more of a saver and he is more of a spender—even though I am the Popular Sanguine and he is the Perfect Melancholy. I was taught to be responsible with money from a very early age and have owned my own business most of my adult life. I have had to be responsible. Because of the differences in spending, Chuck and I have kept our finances separate with agreed-upon shared expenses. This approach has worked well for us and might be a good solution for couples who share this dilemma. You could agree on how much would be put away for college each month—or whatever the agreed upon expense is—and put that into a joint savings account; or better yet, into a CD or money market account where the funds are not easily accessible and where both signatures are needed for a withdrawal. Once the savings funds are put away and the joint expenses met, each could spend or save as they see fit—removing the sense of one partner parenting the other. (Note: here separate accounts are not a trust issue, as they are in the previous chapter, but rather a matter of practicality due to different money management patterns.)

Begin to Budget

Maxine Marsolini, author of *Blended Families,* often encounters couples with problems similar to Bruce and Janna's. If you are in a comparable circumstance, her advice will help you:

> Begin by forming a budget you can live with, not one that is too rigid. If you married a man who is more fun-loving than you, you can't take that quality out of him and have a happy camper. Instead use wisdom. Build a budget [together] that allows him spending within reasonable limits and still makes room for your tendency to save for future goals. This way, you will both feel respected and loved, while keeping alive the spark that drew you to that person in the beginning.

This approach has worked for Chuck and me and it worked for Alicia and Greg—a contributing couple. Their situation is similar to Bruce and Janna's in that Alicia is the conservative one and Greg the spender. Alicia says,

> When Greg and I got married, I brought much more money into the marriage than he had ever thought of having. Not only that, but Greg was still paying off a significant loan to his father from the debt he incurred from his first marriage. We decided to keep everything separate—separate checking and saving accounts; we split all the bills. However, about two and a half years into our marriage, I felt that I was to trust my husband to get to the next level. I wasn't showing him complete trust and he wasn't taking pride in the money I had.

Alicia took a leap of faith giving Greg virtually everything. They combined their accounts and Greg now takes care of the checkbook and the bills. He is in charge of their finances, though Alicia still makes sure they record every expenditure they make. Alicia describes their system:

> We each have a piece of paper and a pencil in our wallets. When the money goes out, it is recorded. At the end of each month, I itemize all the expenses and the income for each month. It then goes on a graph to show where we are. Surprisingly, it has worked wonderfully. We see exactly where our money is going. For instance, Greg's incremental charges on fast food can add up to $100 a month. Once he knows that, he can decide for himself if it is really worth it. When it comes to big expenses, we pray about it together before we make a decision.

They agree it has been a good experience for both of them. Alicia has learned a lesson in trust. Greg has learned to take more responsibility of his money.

They had been married several years and reached a place where Greg had demonstrated financial responsibility with his own finances before he took over their accounts. If they had not reached this level, it would have been foolish to give Greg charge of their bookkeeping. If your marriage is similar to Bruce and Janna's, you might start with budgeted, separate accounts, and later, if you agree it is the right choice, you could try what Alicia and Greg have done. Remember that each marriage relationship is shaped differently. Each has its own equilibrium and no one answer will fit every situation.

Unhealthy Cycle

Chuck sees that Bruce and Janna are in a cycle that they must stop before applying any of these practical ideas. Bruce resents that Janna is unavailable so he spends money to get even. As their funds are drained, Janna works harder to make more money and is gone more. Bruce's resentment grows, and therefore he spends even more. If this sounds like what goes on in your marriage, realize that you are in this cycle. You can brainstorm solutions to break it and then apply some practical money management techniques.

Shared Activities

In reviewing Bruce and Janna's situation, both Chuck and Georgia Shaffer were concerned about the apparent lack of time they spend together doing things they both enjoy—"fun time together," as Georgia called it. She sees that Bruce and Janna are moving apart by playing or working and that each will have to give up some of what they are doing to make a real go of it as a couple. Georgia suggests that Janna may need to put off school or cut back on her hours so there is more time for them as a couple and Bruce will need to limit his time with his buddies.

Chuck agrees that they need to spend more time in joint activities. He recommends that Bruce begin taking classes now, even if it is only one class a term and that Janna become a part of the "boys'" activities. Even if what they do together is not something she enjoys, she can participate by bringing them lunch or a favorite snack or showing an interest in what they are doing.

Chuck has a buddy with whom he likes to build stuff, especially welding. At one point they were working on a carriage for a cannon barrel they bought together. While I have no interest in learning to weld, I can still be involved. I stopped by to check on their progress. Sometimes I brought them cookies while they were working. When Chuck got home, I asked him about it.

Chuck and I have activities we do together, those we do individually, and those we share even though we would not do them without the other person. Chuck loves to mountain bike. While I find that going up and down via the power of my legs is no fun, I did buy a mountain bike so we could ride together. If he wants to ride in the foothills, he goes while I am out of town or am busy. However, I do enjoy taking the ski chairlift to the top of the mountain and riding my bike down. I also enjoy riding on the flat trail that runs along the Rio Grande. So we do those together. Chuck likes to scuba dive. I prefer to lie on the beach with a good book. However, I am a certified scuba diver. When we vacation near the water, we scuba dive together. I like to sail. But unless we have good strong winds giving us forward momentum, Chuck has a tendency to get sick. (He has learned to watch what he eats and to drink plenty of water before we go sailing.) We like to take one sailing trip a year. We each give a little and we have a lot of fun together!

Chuck says that if the husband is placed in a position where he has to choose between his wife and his friends, she can only lose. Either he chooses his wife and harbors resentment, or worse he chooses his friends! Always leave a way out. Therefore, Chuck would encourage anyone in Janna's place to be a part of her husband's circle of friends whenever possible.

If Bruce and Janna's situation sounds like your marriage, take to heart the advice of the peers and professionals offered here. Be willing to make some changes in both your attitudes and behaviors and you are bound to see some improvement in your relationship.

The Interactions

For couples in a similar situation to Janna and Bruce, Chuck would assign the following "homework" assignment:

1. Restructure your finances with the involvement of a bookkeeper or financial planner. Agree upon how much each spouse needs monthly for personal expenses and for joint expenses, with the remainder going toward savings, or another mutually agreed upon plan. The third party is important, as this will remove the spouse from the cop or parent position.
2. Develop and agree on short- and long-term goals, including future education plans. Once goals are established, determine how much must be set aside to achieve them within the desired time frame. The bookkeeper may be needed to keep them on track.
3. In every case, when you are seeking a change in your spouse, ask yourself, "What is the currency that my spouse values?" For example, the currency for Janna is clearly money; however, this is not the case for Bruce. Janna probably assumes that money is of equal value to Bruce. Based on the personality profile found in this couple, we can assume that Bruce values peace, harmony, and fun. In light of this difference, Chuck would attempt to create a "behavior exchange" or barter. If Bruce will agree to certain specific changes, i.e., spend $20 dollars less a week, she will quit nagging him and engage in at least one fun activity a week. Building on the exchange, couples can brainstorm a list of creative ways to save money and a list of ways to bring peace, harmony, and fun into their time together. On a daily basis each should independently record how often each idea was used. Weekly, they will get together and review progress.

Twelve

Secret Spending

Agreement on Expenditures, Establishing Trust, Children from a Previous Marriage

The Issue

Joe and Cindy have been married a few years. Joe is used to people loving him and caring for him. With his Popular Sanguine/Peaceful Phlegmatic personality he has charmed people all his life and they have covered for him. Joe left his first wife, the mother of his children, in search of more fun. As a result of the divorce, Joe lost his position as a pastor and got a job in the business world.

Later, at work, he met Cindy. She is sharp, aggressive, and a leader—everything his wife was not. Joe was immediately attracted to Cindy, a strong Powerful Choleric with some Perfect Melancholy. Cindy, in her late forties, has never been married before; she has been a professional woman all her adult life.

Most of Joe's funds go to support his four children. As a result, he lives from paycheck to paycheck. Cindy's income covers the majority of their living and leisure costs.

Joe knew better than to leave his wife and children. He is plagued with guilt. Cindy feels that his children take advantage of his guilt.

When his oldest daughter called him to ask for a high school graduation party at a local restaurant—which he would pay for—he gave in even though he could not afford it and could not have afforded it even before the divorce. (Such extravagances were not a part of their lifestyle. Things like big parties didn't happen on his pastor's salary.) Since he has no available cash, he borrowed money from his boss to pay for the party and paid it back a little each paycheck.

He made the commitment to his daughter without discussing it with Cindy, as he knew she would say no. By having the money taken out of his paycheck, he thought Cindy would never know. Of course, eventually Cindy found out and she was furious. Not only was Joe's behavior deceptive, but he promised to pay for the party when he could not even contribute significantly to their joint expenses.

Two years later, it was time for the next daughter to graduate. In testing her father's love, she wanted a bigger party at a nicer restaurant. Again, he felt guilty and gave in. Remembering the last blow up, Joe did not tell Cindy. He knew she would be angry again. When the credit card bill came, he took money from their joint account to pay it—again without telling Cindy. Cindy found out when she attempted to take some money from the account and discovered that it had been depleted. Once again, Joe's behavior was deceptive.

Cindy is at her wit's end. She has always been fiscally responsible and is used to having cash at her disposal. She is ready to send Joe back to his original family—who doesn't want him back.

The Insights

The obvious issue that comes into play in this situation is finances, more specifically agreeing on expenditures; this is often a problem in second marriages and especially when there are children from previous marriages involved. Another problem Joe and Cindy face—which we will look at separately—is the issue of trust and respect, something lacking in many marriages. If their story has any similarity to yours, read on.

Agreement on Expenditures

Like Joe and Cindy's saga, Diana and her husband, Mike, also had to address financial issues in relationship to their marriage and their stepchildren. She says,

> I am the mother of two adult children and stepmother to my husband's two adult children from his first marriage. In our seven years of marriage, we have had to come to agreement regarding financing college educations, weddings, and other needs in our children's lives.

The key thing to realize here is that Diana and Mike "have come to an agreement." This is an area apparently lacking in Joe and Cindy's situation. To avoid problems like those described, couples in this place need to address what is realistic for their situation and agree to make decisions together.

Diana continues,

> I married Mike and his children. His financial responsibility for his children became my financial responsibility. Mike married my children and me. My financial responsibility for my children became Mike's. In fact, my daughter was still a minor when we married, so Mike provided shelter, food, and clothing for her because she lived with us. We assisted Mike's son with his advanced education (paid for from shared funds) as well as jointly contributing financially to my son's wedding. Mike's son is getting married next year and we will again be contributing jointly toward those expenses. Each situation is discussed individually.

Consider Personality Differences

One perspective is that since Cindy is more skilled financially, Joe might consider turning over all of the management of their funds to her. The problem with this option is that there is already a tendency for resentment in their marriage. If financial issues are not clearly agreed upon as Diana brought up, Joe is apt to feel dominated and controlled by Cindy, creating an imbalance of power. This is apt to make Cindy the scapegoat for the anger and aggression from the children (and ex-spouse) who are no longer able to manipulate Joe by playing on his guilt/insecurities as a father. For this approach to work, both spouses need to clearly agree that all financial decisions are made together and make it known to the children that this is their parent's decision, not blaming it on the other spouse.

Roseanne Elling, LPC, says,

> When there is an imbalance of power in a marriage, the relationship often resembles that of parent-child rather than of husband-wife. In the case of the Powerful Choleric wife and Peaceful Phlegmatic or Popular Sanguine husband, the wife seems parental (scolding, disapproving) to the less powerful personalities and the husband seems childlike (fearful, irresponsible) to the more powerful personalities. This certainly occurs regardless of gender, but it is most frustrating to a Powerful Choleric wife who longs for a partner, not a dependant. It's difficult to achieve intimacy in a relationship with an "I'm superior/more powerful; you're inferior/less able" underlying attitude.

Separate Finances

Another practical option would be to separate their finances with an agreed upon amount going toward joint expenses. One couple figured out their individual share of payments based on a percentage of their incomes. Using this approach, anything remaining would be available for additional expenses like the graduation parties. You may do something similar—using a percentage of income to determine percentage of contribution—or any other system both of you agree to. Agreeing is the important part.

This is what Chuck and I have done. In fact, to remove the control issues, we have involved a third party. We have a bookkeeper who pays all our bills from a joint checking account. She then tells us how much we each need to contribute to that account. I write a check from my personal account and Chuck writes a check from his. Our checks are then deposited into the joint account to cover the checks written against it. Neither Chuck nor I touch the joint checkbook—though we are both signers on the account. By having the third party involved, I am not telling Chuck what to do and he is not telling me what to do. Control does not become the issue. (If hiring a bookkeeper isn't an option, a trusted friend with a sense for numbers might provide the same service.)

As long as we both contribute as agreed to the joint expenses, neither of us fusses at the other about our personal spending habits. Chuck is apt to buy classic motorcycles or car parts. I am likely to bring home a new outfit when I do not need one. As long as we both meet our agreed upon obligations, these additional expenditures are not an issue. Again, the fact that we have discussed this and agreed upon the solution is paramount to the success of our approach.

Establishing Trust

Another concern seen in our case history is trust and respect. Cindy cannot currently trust Joe, as his pattern has been to do things behind her back. Gaylen Larson, PhD, addresses the importance of trust for this situation.

> Joe needs to realize that he is eroding trust in the marriage by his actions, causing Cindy to think, "If I can't trust him with finances, in what other areas should I not trust him?" Eventually, she will not respect him, which is a primary need. The result could easily be another divorce.

> Joe probably doesn't mean to lie, rather he is trying to avoid a consequence. As a Popular Sanguine/Peaceful Phlegmatic, Joe wants everyone to be happy with him. He gives in to his children rather than disappoint them. He doesn't tell Cindy what he has done because he hopes she will never find out, thus avoiding her wrath. Joe needs to

develop some backbone. He needs to grow up and accept responsibility. Discussing expenditures with Cindy will help in this area as well. The author of *Blended Families,* Maxine Marsolini, says,

> We must realize that surprises with a negative financial impact are really untold truths. When they are discovered they speak volumes about the character of the spouse. Undisclosed truths say our self-image is too fragile to entrust to our mate. In marriage, that is not a good thing.
>
> A wife or husband who discovers hidden financial issues should begin to pray for wisdom, and praise God that the secrets have surfaced. As ugly as it may seem, the truth is about to set you free. Then together commit to finding a small group financial study as is offered through Crown Financial Ministries (www.crown.org), and submit to the godly counsel your family so badly needs. These studies deal not only with budgets, but with honesty, family, respect, delayed gratification, and more.

The combination of societal expectations and gender roles typically taught in the church makes Joe and Cindy's problem very difficult. In marriages where the female is the Powerful Choleric and the male is the Peaceful Phlegmatic, as is at play in our case couple, respect versus resentment is apt to build. Because the Powerful Choleric so naturally takes charge of things—usually doing a better job than the Peaceful Phlegmatic would—it is very easy to just let the Powerful Choleric female take over. While this seems like an easy option in the short run, it creates resentment in the long term.

In this case, Cindy cannot respect Joe because she sees him as weak—giving in to his children's demands and being afraid to discuss it with her first. She is already building resentment toward him because she sees that he is not an adequate provider. This is where Diana's comments about accepting his previous financial obligations as her own are so important.

If Joe is willing to mature to the point that he can address the financial concerns and come to an agreement that he can stick with, Cindy will be able to respect him more, thus lessening the resentment she feels about his contributions toward their joint expenses. For the marriage to succeed, both partners need to be able to respect each other, as Shellie reminds us:

> Stephen and I have learned that respect begins when we admit not only our own weaknesses but also the other's strengths, and decide to draw from those strengths. I am generally better at keeping track of financial things, while Stephen is better at looking at our schedule commitments. We have decided to use those strengths in each other for the betterment of our relationship. He depends on me to keep track of money, and I depend on him to help me see when I have over-committed and am doing too much. What were, at the beginning of our marriage, areas of great frustration have become—after almost fifteen years of marriage—true strengths.

Children from a Previous Marriage

This scenario also presents the possibility of the children trying to sabotage their father's (though it could happen to the mother in a new marriage as well) new marriage. While Joe should not have divorced his first wife, he did. He is now committed in a new relationship and it is too late to go back and undo what has been done. In his book *Sacred Marriage*, Gary Thomas says,

> If you are reading this and you've already gone through a divorce, you serve no one—least of all God—by becoming fixated on something you can't undo. That's what forgiveness and grace are for—a fresh start, a new beginning.[1]

Making his new marriage work must be a priority. Joe needs to accept God's forgiveness for his sin against his first family. Some pastoral counseling might help him with this spiritual truth that, as a former pastor, he must know, yet can't claim. Once he does this, he needs to live as one who is forgiven, not under guilt. Then he will be able to recognize and rightly respond to the manipulative behavior of his children.

Stand Together

Chuck sees that Joe is in the middle between Cindy and his children. Chuck advises that Joe must de-triangulate himself. When issues such as the graduation parties come up, a husband in this place must let the children know that his new wife's input will be sought. He might respond with something like: "Let me check with my wife." If, for example, Joe and Cindy jointly decide that such extravagance is not feasible, as we discussed earlier, Joe then needs to be careful that he does not tell the children that Cindy will not let him have the money. The response needs to be presented as a united decision: "That is not something that we can do right now."

Giving her professional insights, Roseanne Elling adds,

> Stepfamilies and blended families have so many touchy issues. In addition to Joe and Cindy discussing finances in general and specifically, they could possibly agree on an amount they could afford to give his daughter to put toward a graduation party, or whatever she decided to do. It's hard to tell if his daughters are trying to manipulate him, which is very possible, or if they desperately want him in their lives and are resorting to money to find assurance that he cares about them. If a parent is absent from a child's life, he or she will often "settle" for material things just to get some kind of commitment from that parent.

If Joe and Cindy can discuss their finances and reach agreement before issues arise, if they can address the trust and respect concerns typical of their personality combination in marriage, and if Joe can let go of the guilt and de-triangulate from his children, they will be able to get beyond the immediate crisis and begin to build a strong and healthy marriage.

What about you? Are there factors in common with Joe and Cindy's marriage and yours? What can you learn from their situation?

The Interactions

For couples in a similar situation to Joe and Cindy, Chuck would assign the following "homework" assignment:

1. Tackle the struggle with guilt. Whichever spouse is plagued with feelings of guilt, should do this by clearly writing out the actions for which he (or she) is guilty. In order to gain forgiveness, he must take each item listed to the Lord in prayer and confess it. First John 1:9 tells us, "But if we confess our sins, he will forgive our sins, because we can trust God to do what is right. He will cleanse us from all the wrongs we have done." (NCV)
2. Once he obtains forgiveness from God, he must go to the parties he has wronged, his ex-wife and family, and ask their forgiveness for the specific issues. Whether they grant forgiveness is not as important as him asking for it. Coming to his family for forgiveness will validate any feelings they have toward him and may defuse anger. The final step is for him to forgive himself, which is often the hardest aspect of forgiveness. Only once he has dealt with his sins will he be able to focus on the true needs of his children without being motivated by guilt.
3. The husband/father needs to facilitate a family meeting with him, his daughters, and his wife. The purpose of this meeting is to get him out from between his children and spouse. At the meeting, advise the children that all future decisions, especially those regarding money, will be made with his wife. They should not expect an immediate response to their requests.
4. The couple needs to exchange trust for respect. For example, as a Peaceful Phlegmatic, Joe needs respect. When he proves himself to be trustworthy, Cindy will be able to respect him. To make this happen, a man in Joe's place needs to commit to keeping his wife fully informed. Additionally, he needs to take his place as the spiritual leader in the home. As he gets right with the Lord, his temptation to hide things, in essence lying, will be displaced by the active relationship with God. Chuck has found that the wife's desire for the husband to be an active spiritual leader in the

home is common. When working to eradicate a bad behavior, it is easier if it is replaced with a good one. In this case the deception is replaced with spiritual leadership.
5. In our presenting problem, the wife has been focused on the husband's weaknesses. As a result he has been distancing himself from her to the point of hiding things. If this is your case, you should begin to shift your focus from what is wrong with him to what is right. Start by writing down what originally attracted you to him. Once you become more conscious of his qualities, look for them on a daily basis and praise him when those qualities are evident. As he begins to make changes for the better, actively identify what is right and praise him for it. This is where a basic understanding of the personalities will be especially valuable. With the personality combination presented in our case study, the husband's personality will respond much better to praise than to criticism.

PART 4
Ex-Spouse Issues

Thirteen

An Excess of Ex's

External Pressures from the Ex,
Potential Ministry to the Ex

The Issue

This is Jim and Jayne's second marriage each. They each had been married about twenty years before and now have been married for nine years. They have discussed many areas of a second marriage but not what they would do if one of their ex-spouses became seriously ill and expected death. They are now faced with that issue.

Jim's ex-wife is dying of cancer and probably has only a couple of months to live. She is not a Christian and has put the responsibility of all of the decisions about dying and what to do on her older son, a young adult. Jim is struggling with how to help his son without sounding as if he is telling him what to do. The marriage problems with his first wife originally revolved around Jim's faith. He is a devoted Christian and she didn't want anything to do with it. In the meantime, the son wants to do the right thing, but he is in a dilemma of what that would be.

Jayne, a Christian, observes the situation from the sidelines, which is difficult for her take-charge Powerful Choleric personality. She wants to help and support both her stepsons to let them know she cares, without making them feel she is mothering them. It is hard for them to see

Christ's love through Jayne since they are not believers, even though they go to church.

Additionally, Jayne wants to minister to her husband. She is sure he is experiencing a loss there, but she doesn't know how to address it. After all, the ex-wife is the mother of his children.

Jim is open to discussing how he feels about his ex-wife dying. He says it is going to be a loss because she was a part of his life, and they brought two boys into this world together. However, he does not have any personal feelings about her because that was in the past and those feelings died a long time ago.

Jim and Jayne both want the sons and the grandchildren to know how much they love them. Jim knows what a loss it will be for his boys because he lost his father at an early age. Yet, as the stepmother, Jayne doesn't know how to deal with the children and grandchildren. Does she say anything to the grandchildren, ages five and three, that their grandmother will not be in heaven because she is not a believer?

At the same time, Jayne's ex-husband's wife has contacted her. Jayne's ex-husband has committed adultery once again. His wife is not a believer and she is very bitter and angry about what has happened. While Jayne feels compassion for this woman, she doesn't feel that it is her problem.

Jim and Jayne discussed many things prior to marriage, but neither ever thought of these complications. Each feels stressed by circumstances that are totally out of their control. Although Jim and Jayne feel that God put them together and wants them to have the best marriage ever, they'd like to run away from the issues, which may mean running away from each other.

The Insights

The story of Jim and Jayne has a lot going on that most people in a second marriage do not think about. It is easy to be so absorbed in your own issues and the immediate struggles of making the marriage work that you do not think about the "what if's." This situation brings the reality of those things to light. While there are several concerns at work here, the key issues involve how the current spouse feels. As Jim and Jayne are the ones currently married to one another, their marriage must take priority. As a loving and caring Christian individual, Jayne can be a comfort to both of the other women in this scenario, but only as much as Jim feels is appropriate and only if her involvement is not a stress in their marriage.

Examine your own marriage and see if there are issues you did not anticipate. Your issues may be different from the case couple's, but some of the suggestions are apt to help you see your own problems in a new light.

External Pressures from the Ex

The best thing for Jim and Jayne is to keep in mind that the stresses they face are both external, meaning they are not created within the marriage, and they are not eternal, but temporal.

Jim's ex-wife is dying. This is a concern that will not last forever. The question is, will Jim and Jayne handle it in such a way that it is a growth experience or one that will harbor resentment for years to come? The crisis of Jayne's ex-husband's wife's trauma will move on as well.

Georgia Shaffer, Pennsylvania licensed psychologist and author of *A Gift of Mourning Glories,* suggests Jim continue to keep the lines of communication open with Jayne.

> Grieving begins with the loss of his ex-wife's health and will continue for months after her death. It could take years until Jim, his children, and grandchildren fully adjust and rebuild. In the meantime, Jayne must remind herself that grieving is not a situation that can be fixed but a process to be worked through. Jayne needs to give Jim permission to grieve over the loss of his children's mother and realize that intense feelings of sadness and anger can be a part of it.
>
> Jayne also needs to be reminded that the reason grieving lasts far longer than most of us expect is because we can only handle a small amount of pain at a time. It's a lot like opening the lid and letting the pressure off a shaken bottle of soda and then closing it, Jim will have times when the death of his ex-wife will be real and painful, and then he will have times when

it doesn't affect his day at all. But slowly over time, Jim will come to the place of accepting that the mother of his children will no longer be involved in their lives.

Are there external pressures that threaten your present relationship? If so, what can you do to de-pressurize them? Are they temporary or long-term problems? Do they need to be addressed now or will they pass with time?

Help the One Who Hurts

First, a spouse in Jayne's situation needs to take her husband's welfare into consideration. You should be supportive of his feelings of loss and grief. This is not the time for you to feel threatened by the ex-wife—even if you have been in the past. The ex-wife won't be an issue in the future unless your attitude forces your husband to keep his feelings hidden. Acting defensive, jealous, and threatened are apt to signal to your husband that he cannot discuss his ex-wife with you. Be a good listener and only offer advice when asked. Despite your love and care for them, you'll be an outsider in this situation. If Jayne were to attempt to limit Jim or his sons' connection with the ex-wife/mother, it would only result in long-term resentment on their parts.

If Jayne's advice is asked, she might suggest that Jim's son get some outside support in the care of his mother.

Michelle Holman, MA, LPC, encourages Jim's son to seek help,

> Whether it be at his church or with others who face losing a parent to cancer, he should have some outside support. This will enable him to make wise decisions, not only for his mother, but ones to protect his current family as well.

Take the High Road

In looking at the situation with Jim's ex-wife, Jayne needs to ask herself, "What would be the best-case scenario here?" Chuck suggests that Jayne can only win by taking the high road. While the scenario doesn't allude to it, one can assume that there is bound to be some contentiousness between Jayne and the ex-wife. At the least, their disagreement may have to do with their faith. On the other extreme, they may have battled over holidays, alimony, and custody.

Chuck suggests that the optimum outcome might be for Jim's ex-wife to give Jayne her blessing, to say to the children and grandchildren, "I want you to know, you have my blessing to make Jayne *the* grandmother for your children. Please know that you can go to her in times of need. Jayne and I are at peace and we want you to be as well."

With this as a goal, a wife in this situation should start by sharing her concerns with her husband and asking his permission to visit his ex-wife. Assuming this is acceptable, your aim is to bury the hatchet and offer to reconcile. As a wife who wants to make this adjustment as painless as possible for your husband, you must start by apologizing for anything negative that may have gone on between you and the ex-wife. Even if the ex-wife is clearly more at fault, you have nothing to gain by holding out. Hopefully the ex-wife will turn around and apologize as well. But, if she doesn't, you will have the peace of knowing that you have done the right thing.

Psychologist Georgia Shaffer, says,

> Jayne can also serve and support her husband's ex by asking her if there are any letters or small gifts she would like to leave behind. Jayne could gather writing paper, assist with the letter writing, or purchase a few special mementos. Any small thing that would help ease the final separation for the family would be a real gift to them. Unfortunately, Jayne may also have to put her social life on hold during this difficult time. Dinner parties, weekend trips may have to be postponed. When one person has cancer, it affects the lives of all involved. If Jayne can compassionately endure these short-term losses, her marriage will become something even better.

Audrey faces a similar situation: her husband's ex-wife is dying, though the children are younger. She has become friends with this woman and helps out in any way she can. She says,

I am a friend to the children, but I do not try to mother them. I am sure when she dies the children will be able to come to me for comfort and support. If my neighbor was sick, I would do the same for her. Why should it be any different just because she is my husband's ex-wife?

For everyone in a similar situation, if your first efforts are received positively, you might ask the ex-wife if there are any dreams for her children or grandchildren that you can help fulfill. The dying mother may have always wanted to see her son go to law school or to have her grandchild take piano lessons. For example, it could be a comfort to Jim's ex-wife to know that Jayne would be willing to encourage the son by working in his business while he goes to school. To help facilitate the grandchild's piano lessons, Jayne might agree that when he is old enough, she will pick him up from school, take him to and from his lessons, listen to him practice, and attend his recitals. Some of the estate could be set aside to help achieve these goals.

What can you do to take the higher road in your present situation with an ex-spouse? Your first priority is your present relationship. This relationship might be improved by treating an "ex" with greater respect.

Potential Ministry to the Ex

With Jim's permission and the success of these preliminary steps, Jayne could share Christ with her new friend. However, this may be a place better filled by Jim. Eva Marie shares,

> Were I Jim, I would contact the ex and ask for the opportunity to talk with her. This is where I failed. The Lord spoke to my heart four years before my ex died. He had told me that my ex was dying and that I needed to call him. I refused the call. When I got the word that John had died, I grieved as much for my stupidity as for his loss and the loss of his family.

Melanie Wilson, PhD, suggests that Jim and Jayne reach out in any way the ex-wife is willing to let them, including taking her into their home.

> Her soul is what is important now; love and self sacrificing are the best witnessing tools.

Whether or not she responds favorably to Jayne's witness must not influence the positive relationship Jayne has worked to develop with her.

Preserve Precious Memories

Additionally, as the outsider, it is not Jayne's place to tell any of the family members that their mother/grandmother is hell-bound. Michelle Holman agrees. She says,

> It is not constructive to tell the grandchildren that their grandmother is going to hell. Instead, continue to encourage and model an authentic relationship with Jesus for them. Let them see the difference He can make in life.

Sherrie shares the following peer insight. This is what happed in a similar situation when her stepchildren's grandmother passed away.

> Bob's boys' unsaved grandmother passed away. Their mom, Bob's ex, asked us to pray for her, and when she died family members referred to her as being in a "better place." The boys were old enough to figure out that their grandmother didn't profess Jesus as Lord and probably wasn't in heaven. But they didn't and couldn't accept the weight of that likelihood so we never discussed it. Bob and I figured they would come to some determination about that when they were mature enough to consider it fully. At any rate, had we "informed" them, it would have added cruel weight to their loss. To inform anyone of their loved one's eternal destiny is walking on shaky ground, especially with children of such a young age. Children don't have

the ability to process that concept of God's nature—justice. I would advise Jayne to continue to reinforce that God loves their grandmother very much and offer to pray for her with them.

While there is no way to ensure success, one can hope that Jayne's actions will result in both women being at peace with each other. This will free the children to develop an ongoing relationship with Jayne without feeling that they are being disloyal to their dead mother.

Is there anyone in your situation who needs the touch of a Christian spirit? Perhaps you can reach out to someone who does not understand God's forgiveness. This is truly an example of going beyond our natural human tendencies to a level of giving, not getting—love extravagant.

View Them as Neighbors

Audrey mentioned looking at what one might do if a neighbor was facing a difficult time. With this in mind, we look at the situation of Jayne's ex-husband's new wife. Unless Jayne has had an ongoing relationship with her, Jayne is under no obligation to help out in the situation, and should not if Jim is threatened by Jayne's involvement. For example, talking with her ex-husband's new wife and discussing his adultery could agitate Jayne's past issues and impact her relationship with Jim. As Jim is her priority, he must be taken into consideration first.

The peers who have provided insights throughout the book had mixed feelings on this complicated issue. Shellie offered her thoughts:

> Outside of a definite word from God that this is the time to establish a spiritual relationship with and mentor the new wife, Jayne should not actively pursue this right now. She should not put herself in a mentoring position when her husband and the family need so much of her time, energy, attention, and prayers.

In contrast, Karen sees that

> Jayne has a real opportunity here to make a difference in lives by living and loving with Christ's incomparable love. What an

incredible testimony to her faith in Christ when she's able to really transcend the normal human response and reach out to her ex-husband's new wife.

While there is no clear-cut answer to this aspect of the situation, if Jim is okay with Jayne comforting her ex-husband's wife and she can do it without it creating emotional turmoil in her own life and marriage, Jayne should do what she can to help. If someone in her church was facing the same difficulty and Jayne had experience with it, she wouldn't hesitate to get involved. Though, due to the complex nature of the situation, she ought to establish some boundaries such as Jayne's former relationship with the ex is off-limits, and Jayne's effort to comfort a woman going through the same thing she has experienced must not become a "beat up on the ex" time.

In Scripture we are advised to comfort others,

> He comforts us every time we have trouble, so when others have trouble, we can comfort them with the same comfort God gives us. (2 Corinthians 1:4 NCV)

While Jayne seemed to be unfairly faced with ex-spouse issues on both sides, as a Christian she needs to look at both of these women as women, not as enemies. Everyone involved needs compassion and understanding. As a Christian, Jayne has an opportunity to love extravagantly, not to get, but to give.

The Interactions

For couples with any aspect of Jim and Jayne's situation, select the following "homework" assignments that fit your needs:

1. In the presenting problem, the wife's primary responsibility is to meet her husband's needs. Whatever she does in relation to his family members needs to be within the range of his wishes. The situation may be flipped in your house. Whichever the case, discuss the various options presented within the chapter to see

which of the possible situations would be appropriate in your situation. For example, with his approval, the wife could meet with each of the family members individually to ask how she can be most helpful to them. If he asks her to stay out of it, she must be content with that option.
2. The spouse serving as the support system should read *Roses in December* by Marilyn Heavilin to gain an understanding of how each personality grieves differently.
3. The family should go to grief therapy to help them work through the stages of grief and the unique aspects of this situation.
4. Even in ministry, any involvement with the spouse of the ex should only be done after a discussion with the current spouse to determine what level of involvement is mutually acceptable.

Fourteen

Deep Resentment on a Delicate Subject

Attitude Adjustment, Guided by Guilt

The Issue

Darren and Louise have now been married for about eight years. As a part of his divorce settlement, he agreed to pay his former wife half of what his annual income was then for as long as she lives. At the time, Darren was flying high. He had just had his best year ever. His commitment to his ex-wife is more than many entire families live on—$3000 every month.

However, his industry has faced severe setbacks and Darren's income is not what it once was. The settlement did not allow for any changes in his income. While some might think there should have been a decreasing clause or that she should become independent of him, no such provisions were made. Darren felt sorry for her and feels guilty for divorcing her.

While Darren's current income is adequate to support him, it is not enough to support both him and Louise—let alone the ex-wife. Louise is a hard worker and expected to work when she married Darren, even though his income was higher when they married. However, Louise has grown weary of the situation. She feels that she must work as hard as she does just to pay the ex-wife—who lives alone and does not work and has no car to maintain. Darren and Louise's expenses vary greatly from hers. Louise feels it is unfair that the ex-wife can live at this comfortable level while she and Darren have to watch their budget closely.

Darren has no intention of reopening this issue in court. In fact, at the time of the divorce, he did not have an attorney represent him. He wanted to get it over and gave her the house, car (later sold), and half of his income for life.

Louise has learned not to bring up this delicate subject. Sometimes she's pretty good about accepting the situation; other times she deeply resents this financial agreement. Louise is doing her best to leave it with God, but it's *so hard!*

The Insights

Payments to ex-spouses are a volatile issue, and your view may depend heavily on which side of the question your experience lies. Some may quickly jump to the side of Darren's ex-wife, believing that she deserves anything she can get because Darren broke his promise to her by divorcing her. In that case, Louise has no grounds for complaint.

On the flip side, we do not know the circumstances of the divorce. We do know from the information provided that Darren feels guilty for divorcing his ex-wife. It is possible that he is a man of principle and, despite all the things that may have played into the divorce, he feels responsible. By today's standards, Darren's monthly payments are high and providing them for life is uncommon. If the payer's income changes, payments are often adjusted, up or down.

With that said, since without complete details either response could be appropriate—and your situation may include either side—we have chosen to look at both sides as possible options.

If Chuck were seeing Darren and Louise as clients, he would meet with them individually to see who might be more receptive to changing their position, as a resolution will require some compromise. In most relationships, one party is more willing to be flexible, to give, while the other is more resistant to change. The scenario suggests that Louise has accepted her need to adjust, and that Darren "has no intention of reopening the issue in court," making him the more rigid. However, in your situation, the tables could be turned. In order to make this chapter beneficial to the most couples, we will address each side as if it is the one to yield. When each spouse is prepared to be the one to change, a compromise is easier to reach. A good premise to work from is the "change first principle": each person takes responsibility for change, regardless of what the other person does. Conversely, human nature is to meet halfway, which often results in a stalemate.

Attitude Adjustment: What Louise Can Do

With the example of our case history couple, Louise has apparently discussed her feelings with Darren and found that he is unwilling to make an adjustment. So she will have to be the one who is willing to flex. This process may involve adjusting her attitude about her husband, his responsibility in the situation, and the money.

If your situation is similar, to fully apply the love extravagantly principle in this situation, you will need to continue to work at, as Louise put it, "going along with it." After all, you did marry knowing the circumstances and knowing that you would have to contribute financially to the union.

In Stephanie and Kurt's situation, she had to deal with similar issues when they married. She reports,

> He had an agreement to pay his ex-wife approximately $75,000 over a six-year period. When we married, he had five years to go. However, due to his alcohol problems and debts, he became delinquent. The payments went into arrears and it seemed like forever until we were out from under this burden. Yes, we lived on a strict budget, and yes, she bought cars and other things we didn't get. The first thing I had to realize is that when you marry someone, there is no his debt or her debt—everything is one.

If Louise's heart attitude is to give, not to get—to love extravagantly—then where the money she contributes to the checking account actually goes will be a non-issue. However, in day-to-day living, that is more easily said than done. As Louise has indicated, some days she does well with it, other days she finds resentment taking over. Here are some practical suggestions to help anyone in a similar situation to Louise make this adjustment.

Adjust Your Focus

Several peer contributors suggested that Louise focus on the good things about Darren. Specifically, Kristi encourages women in Louise's place to focus on the really important issues, instead of the money.

> Ask yourself, "What genuinely good characteristics is he exhibiting in this situation?" He is a man of integrity who does what he agreed to do. He is a man of loyalty who refused to fight it out in court. He is a man of honor who has no intention of drumming up the unpleasant past. You wouldn't be happy at all if he were stingy, unethical, or cruel. Concentrating on those genuinely fine characteristics instead of the negatives will help you maintain a positive attitude.

Melanie Wilson, PhD, agrees. She offers Louise the following professional insight that you can adjust to your situation,

> It appears that you married a passive, Peaceful Phlegmatic man. Although his failure to stand up to his ex-wife causes you some financial and emotional discomfort, I am sure you find his personality attractive in many ways. How does his easy-going personality benefit you? Would you be upset if he suddenly became more controlling and decided to contest the divorce settlement? What if he also started to control you, telling you to get a better-paying job? Focusing on his strengths and realizing that the total package is well worth the difficulties may help.

Accept What You Cannot Control

So Louise could start by adjusting her attitude about Darren. Next she may need to learn to accept the situation as it is. Kathy offers this peer insight:

> In this case, the second wife really has no grounds for complaint. Her husband now was then the husband of the first wife. The guilt he felt was justified—he divorced her. The commitment he gave his wife is the consequence of divorce. Similar to the old adage, "ignorance of the law is no excuse," the breakup of a marriage always has consequences—whether we like it or not. Darren is honoring his word and that is commendable.

The harsh reality is, there are consequences of divorce and Louise did know about them heading into her marriage with Darren. As a result, it is not reasonable for her to expect him to make changes now because she is unhappy with the arrangement. As others have pointed out, Darren is an honorable man to hold to his agreement—which is something few do today. Louise should focus on Darren's strengths and accept her situation.

Additionally, she may need to change her view of the money, as Karen suggests. As both an ex-wife and the new wife, Karen says,

> I think she truly has no option but to honor her husband by accepting his choice. She cannot control it, so she must try to see it differently in order to not harbor resentment. Perhaps she can change her way of thinking. Pretend the money is an unavoidable expense [which it really is], like a health issue. Her effort to accept his decision will pay off in the long run because he will ultimately appreciate her acceptance of his decision.

Make Necessary Lifestyle and Spiritual Changes

Chuck would advise couples facing Louise and Darren's dilemma to adjust their lifestyle to be able to easily live on the total available income of the husband and wife. If that is not sufficient, perhaps, in this case, the husband could take on an additional part-time job or do some consulting work on the side so both feel that he is "providing." Additionally, seeing extra effort may help the wife feel that she is not alone in her hard work and income production.

These suggestions can help you deal with the practical aspects of your situation. Additionally, there is a spiritual element that must be addressed. Like Louise, many of us get so focused on the issue, the trees, that we can't see the bigger picture, the forest. But God sees the whole thing.

Kristi reminds Louise to focus on the Lord.

> He is your real resource for life, not your salary or your husband's.
> He can provide more than enough for both households.

In the Bible study I attend, we were recently talking about God's provision for us. The question came up, "How has God provided for you in a time of need?" I thought of a time when Chuck's employment situation was in turmoil and just making the house payment was a struggle. God did supply, though not in the way I would have chosen. Over a period of a few months I was involved in four minor traffic accidents. Two were my fault. Two were not. My vehicle was not damaged to the point that it had to be repaired to drive, but it was damaged. I received checks from the insurance companies that made a big difference at the time. Miraculously, our insurance was never cancelled! Since that time, our life has stabilized—as has my driving. It has now been years since I've had an accident.

Matthew 6:25–34 is a good reminder of God's provision for all of us. Anyone in a similar situation to Louise might want to focus on verse 33:

> The thing you should want most is God's kingdom and doing what God wants. Then all these other things you need will be given to you. (NCV)

While this will be hard, you can make these adjustments. After all, marriage is more important than worrying about rights or keeping a fairness tally. That is the whole goal of loving extravagantly, not to get, but to give.

Guided by Guilt: What Darren Can Do

While it is easy to point the finger at Louise with a "you-asked-for-it-you-got-it" attitude, there is another side to the story. Chuck would talk to Darren about his duty to his current marriage, to Louise. Did guilt rather than logic, the law, or even reason guide the marital separation agreement?

Addressing her approach to this situation, Michelle Holman, MA, LPC, says,

> I would talk to the husband about praying toward God leading them to a reasonable resolution. I would also ask him to pray that God would reveal any guilt about the divorce associated with his financial support. Often when a spouse just gives in to the other spouse, it is their way of not acknowledging the reality of a failed marriage—which, especially for Christians, is a grief process and takes time and a lot of grace.

Yes, divorce is not God's perfect plan. Yes, it is a sin. Yes, it does have consequences. But the wonderful thing about God is His grace. Assuming that Darren has asked for God's forgiveness for his role in the divorce, he is forgiven. His life does not need to be ruled by guilt. In addressing divorce and remarriage, the notes in my *Women's Study Bible* say,

> With God, forgiveness is as if it never happened. No sin or tragedy is beyond God's forgiveness. After seeking God's forgiveness, which we all do repeatedly, a woman [or man] who remarries has a new understanding of God's incredible grace.[1]

Darren appears to have made a choice based on guilt. While some support may be in order as a consequence, Darren's settlement does appear to be outside the norm, especially today. CPA Reese Gateley says,

> From the financial side, I have never seen an agreement like the one you are describing. Darren has boxed himself into a corner. He never should have represented himself. Guilt [apparently] took over.

Michelle Holman agrees,

> Some states do not even make allowances for alimony.... It's usually only given if the wife has been a stay-at-home mom and needs time to prepare for a career.

Do a Reality Check

Since, based on the information given, we believe Darren is a Peaceful Phlegmatic, we can assume that he may be taking the path of least resistance—choosing peace now while putting off any conflict that would result in long-term contentment. As his therapist, Chuck would confront him with the reality of the situation, telling him, "That's $36,000 a year, $360,000 every ten years. Is that what you want to do?" If Darren hasn't thought this through, Chuck would coach him to take responsibility for doing what's best for the long term—taking care of Louise—and to do it now rather than putting off the unpleasant task. The longer he waits, the deeper the hole. More resentment will build in Louise, and the ex-wife's expectation of ongoing support will be more firmly entrenched.

Chuck would also press for an answer to the question, "Is this fair to Louise? If you were single, without the benefit of Louise's income, would you be able to pay your ex-wife and still live?" Perhaps this reality would help Darren see the situation from Louise's point of view and make him willing to look into making an adjustment.

Investigate Options

From this perspective, Chuck would encourage couples in Darren and Louise's situation to talk to a lawyer who has expertise in these issues in their state—without committing to any change, just to investigate their options. A lawyer may review the case and determine that there is no choice. At this point, the issue will be closed and need not be pursued further. The wife will feel valued knowing that her husband cared enough about her feelings to be willing to make a change, which should help her adjust her attitude, but no change in the agreement will be made.

If a change is possible, then husband and wife will need to spend time in prayer and seek wise counsel as to their next course of action. Making a change is something that can only be determined between them and God. In using our case history couple, Darren may want to consider the fact that if he and his first wife never divorced, she would still have to make adjustments if his income changed.

Chuck would then meet with the couple. He would have each affirm the other's position in mutual submission (Eph. 5:21). The Bible asks husbands and wives to submit to one another out of reverence for Christ—that is each giving 100 percent. For example, Louise would say, "I married you debts and all, and I support you in your commitment to honor your ex-wife." Darren would say to Louise, "I realize I was driven by guilt and have taken the easy path. This has placed an unfair burden on you as my wife. My duty is to do what is best for you now." When each person is willing to go more than half way, it lays the groundwork for a healthy compromise. This takes maturity on the part of both spouses.

In his book *Sacred Marriage*, Gary Thomas says,

> A mature husband and wife can grow leaps and bounds spiritually as they learn to compromise and move toward the other.[2]

If they do decide to proceed with an adjustment in the settlement, Darren and his ex-wife must agree to a change, or they will need to go back to court—which is likely. If Darren is willing to reopen the issue, legal counsel should definitely be sought.

Ideally, both Darren and Louise would be willing to let go a little and they could meet in the middle. In their case, that might mean doing what it takes to make a reasonable adjustment to the marital settlement agreement. If Darren remains resolute, Louise can still make adjustments to her attitude that will make a big difference in their relationship—this is true extravagant love, selfless love, and although it feels like being lost in the trees, it is God's view of the entire forest.

The Interactions

Due to the unique nature of the presenting problem and the differing insights presented to the wife and then to the husband, the homework assignment here is arranged accordingly. If you have similar issues in your marriage, apply these suggestions accordingly.

For the Husband

1. Write ten different statements describing why you feel guilty for having divorced your ex-wife.
2. Evaluate each of the guilt statements. Address whether each one does or does not constitute a legitimate source of guilt in the present. For each current source of guilt, write why it is legitimate.
3. Then, for each source of legitimate guilt, write a response to:
   - Have I asked God for forgiveness? Has God forgiven me?
   - Have I forgiven myself?
   - Have I asked my ex-wife for forgiveness?
   - I can gain forgiveness by _____ .
4. Write a response either agreeing or disagreeing with the statements:
   - Giving money to my ex-wife will earn forgiveness.
   - My duty is to my current wife.

For the Wife

1. Write ten reasons why excessive payments to the ex-wife would reasonably build resentment in you. (This is to begin validating your feelings.)
2. Write down your fears for the present and future. Evaluate each for probability. Share your feelings with your spouse.
3. Write a marital balance sheet, using the format an accountant would use, with the alimony payment as a debit or loss. List on one side all the things that are good with the marriage (assets), both financial and otherwise. An asset might be something as simple as "we have fun together" or "he makes me laugh." On the other side, list all the things that are bad (liabilities). Ideally, this will help put the liability of the alimony in perspective. (If this were a premarital situation, this exercise would help determine if the relationship should continue.)
4. List the things you are asking your husband to do before you can accept the payments to the ex-wife as a business expense with no emotion attached to it. (For example: See a lawyer to look into reduced payments.)
5. List the things you can do in the event your husband makes no changes.

Completing these suggested homework assignments could provide valuable insights for both the husband and wife enabling them to look at their situation objectively. Writing things down—the written word—provides an element of control rather than allowing irrational fears and the "what if's" of uncertainty to gain a stronghold. These new insights could be the framework for creating a new plan of action. With the foundation based on seeking God's best for all parties, a couple would be free to exercise their highest levels of trust and respect necessary to love extravagantly.

Part 5
Stepfamily Issues

Fifteen

Between a Rock and a Hard Place

Disciplining Children, Commitment

The Issue

When Ben and Lucille began dating, she was a widow with two children—a daughter, Nancy, who was in high school and a son, Clay, who was in junior high. Ben included the children in their dates. Though he'd been warned of a possible tug of war for their mother's affections, Ben felt up to the challenge and he didn't hesitate to spend a lot of time with them. On weekends, he frequently took them all on a drive to a location where they could picnic, fish, or take a walk in nature. Many times the day ended with a barbecue.

Ben knew that Lucille's first husband, the father of her children, was abusive and that Lucille and the children still harbored fears from their traumatic experiences. If Ben raised his voice, the children quickly moved toward their mother, as if to protect her. As he continually demonstrated love and consistency—though not perfectly—he gently wooed them, and their fears seemed to evaporate. He tried to use every opportunity to demonstrate to them what a man who loved them should be like. He believed love would conquer all.

Soon after the couple's wedding, Ben started noticing changes in Clay, who flew into a rage when corrected, daring Ben to discipline him—shouting, "You're not my father. You can't tell me what to do." Although Ben and Lucille differed on what should be done, they did what they could to calm and redirect him, but he kept making wrong choices. Ben held a firm hand and Lucille was more lax. One day, the call came from the sheriff that he had Clay in custody and was taking him to juvenile hall.

Arguments between Ben and Lucille about how to deal with Clay have escalated. Ben has begun to wonder if they wouldn't all be better off if he left the marriage. After all, if he stays and can't do anything to stop Clay's waywardness, Ben feels he would be blamed for not doing what he could. But if he leaves, he would be leaving Lucille, whom he loves. He can't stay and he can't go. Each day seems worse. Ben is stuck between a rock and a hard place.

The Insights

While Ben and Lucille's situation does have some complications that make it unique, they also have concerns, struggles, and frustrations that are common to households where two adults with different approaches to discipline live and where teenagers are present. Regardless of the past issues, it is imperative that all couples in a similar situation to Ben and Lucille present a united front. Rebellion in teenagers is a problem that many parents face. In our case history couple, we see that Ben has become a stabilizing factor in Clay's life, and his departure could create additional problems for Clay. Ben needs to honor his commitment.

Disciplining Children

Our scenario indicates that Ben has come into a home accustomed to turbulence and he has a grounding affect: "As he gently wooed them, the fears seemed to evaporate." However, shortly after Ben and Lucille were married, things began to change between Ben and Clay. Ben is making assumptions that Clay resents his presence and that things are getting worse. Although one can clearly see how Ben might jump to this conclusion, Ben needs to remember that Clay brought plenty of his own emotional issues into this new relationship.

Michelle Holman, MA, LPC, sees that this behavior is typical of Clay's situation. She explains,

> One problem that I see over and over again is when a parent has over-bonded with a child because of an absent or abusive spouse. When there is a new marriage/relationship, the child is angry, resentful, and/or jealous of the new connection and doesn't know how to adjust.

This may be the case with Lucille and Clay. For many years, she may have had to protect him from his father. Now that he is older, she doesn't know how to make the adjustment from protecting him to disciplining him. Additionally, in situations when a child loses a parent, he tends to become very possessive of the remaining parent. Anyone new in the home, such as Ben, is bound to generate anxiety. The existing equilibrium is being temporarily thrown off balance.

United Front

We might also assume from the case presented that Ben probably has the stronger personality, and that Lucille is apt to be the more passive of the two. Since Ben has the stronger personality, and is the male, it might be easy for Lucille to give the reins of discipline to Ben. However, that will split the desirable structure of the family. Ben will be above Lucille and the children. Instead, Lucille and Ben need to be peers together in authority above the children. Because Lucille was previously in the role of protector, it is especially important that her children see her and Ben as working together.

Peer advisors, Ruth and Bill, believe that their joining together to deal with her son Jim's anger was central to their success with him. Like Ben, Bill made the decision as to how things should be done, but Ruth totally supported his choice. Looking back on that time, Ruth remembers,

My son Jim's relationship with Bill was very similar to Clay's with Ben—defiance, anger, rejection. We didn't get into police and juvenile hall issues, but I believe that would have happened if Bill and I had not handled things as we did. God gave me the grace to get out of the way and allow Bill to deal with Jim as he believed he should. I backed him up in his decisions about Jim. I did not run interference for either of them.

Ruth reports that today Jim is grown up, self-supporting, and self-sufficient.

Jim calls Bill "Dad" at least part of the time (his choice), asks him for advice (and sometimes even follows it!), turns to him for praise and affirmation, and in general accepts him as his father.

Susan Rogers, MA, LPC, advises parents and stepparents by saying,

It is helpful for the stepmother to say, "These are your dad's rules and I am supporting his wishes." The stepfather can say, 'These are your mother's rules and I am supporting her wishes." This keeps the inevitable argument: "You're not my real parent," at bay.

Additionally, it is not healthy for Lucille's daughter, Nancy—or Clay—to think that only men have power. Lucille must share in the disciplinary action, providing a healthy model for the children to internalize. Avoiding it will set Ben up as the "bad cop"—increasing the children's anger and resentment toward him. While good cop/bad cop may work in interrogating criminals, it is a bad model for raising children.

Don't Expect a "Quick Fix"

Bev, one of our peer advisors, grew up in a situation similar to that of Ben and Lucille's. Her brother, too, had trouble with the law. Her mother was hesitant to come down hard on her brother; after all, he had been through so much—an alcoholic father, desertion, and divorce. By the time Bev's stepfather arrived on the scene, many of the family behavior patterns were firmly established. He had an uphill battle trying to give boundaries to Bev's brother, especially without Bev's mother's support.

Bev reports,

> My mom and stepdad met with a probation officer on a regular basis. My mom gave my stepdad more and more freedom in dealing with my little brother. She could see that her approach was not doing the job. At first my brother was even worse in his behavior at home. He showed his hatred of my stepdad for depriving him of his freedoms when he disobeyed. But, with my mom's support, my stepfather held firm and steady.
>
> It took months, but like a ship being turned by a tug, my brother started changing his behavior. By the end of the year, my brother was making different choices most of the time. My mom followed the lead my stepfather set and stood with him in making my brother accountable. I'd encourage anyone in this situation to do the same.

Georgia Shaffer, Pennsylvania licensed psychologist, agrees.

> So often we grow weary when the situation we are attempting to improve isn't fixed immediately. We gave it our best and quickly conclude that our best wasn't good enough. Clay's problems are a result of many difficult years, and in order to make a lasting change it will likely take much longer than Ben and Lucille have the patience for. They need to continue providing a loving, supportive, and structured environment and focus on God's ability to transform the most hopeless of circumstances.

Chuck sees it as imperative that Ben and Lucille speak with one voice and offers Ben encouragement: "Sometimes when kids finally get into a safe environment, they begin to act out unresolved issues—which need to come out eventually. Clay's behavior could be because he is feeling safe for the first time in his childhood." Clay is bound to have issues with grief, abandonment, and anger. Since the biological father is no longer present, Clay is projecting his feelings about his father onto Ben. In counseling, Chuck has often been the target of a child's anger that was really about, and originated with, his father. Once in a therapeutic setting, the child feels safe expressing these previously pent up emotions.

Richard had similar difficulties with his own son.

> My son lived with his mother until she threw him out when he was thirteen. Eventually, it was up to my new wife and I to try to raise him. We struggled to help him and keep him on the right course—but being his father's son, he had to learn everything the hard way. I was tempted to kick him out many times, and I had plenty of reason: DWI at age sixteen, drugs, getting a girl pregnant. . . . However, every time I was ready to give up, I was reminded by God that what he needed was love. Together my wife and I worked to love this unlovable teenager until he finally did graduate from high school and move out.

Set Boundaries

Couples in Ben and Lucille's situation must stand shoulder to shoulder in their agreed upon discipline and their love for the troubled teen. The boundaries they give are a form of love. While working with violent offenders in a residential treatment center, Chuck found that even violent teens are fearful of an environment where there is no order or control and ultimately respond positively to healthy boundaries.

Finding the balance between showing love and setting boundaries is a difficult task. A good approach is to give the teen as much freedom as his ability to handle responsibility allows. If his actions continue to indicate that he cannot be trusted with responsibility, then his freedoms need to be pulled in, tightening the reigns.

I remember my rebellious teens. Every time I went too far, every time

I messed up, some of my freedoms were taken away. It wasn't that I was grounded or specifically punished—depending on the violation—but next time I asked for permission for something that was questionable, the freedom was denied. If my failures were few and far between, the restrictions on my freedoms were minimal or non-existent. If they were frequent, the boundaries were moved in tighter. I understood this system and often knew that a certain choice would cost me many weeks of earning back my parents' trust.

While not a stepparent herself, Mary Hunt Webb, MA, has faced similar circumstances in the classroom as a college educator. Mary says,

> Boys like Clay are looking for boundaries, and as a result, they crash into them all the time. They must be shown that the boundaries are there and that they will not dissolve—no matter what he does. In situations like this, it is good if Clay can receive consequences for his action from sources outside the home. This way, Clay would not see the consequences as Ben and Lucille punishing him; it would be society telling him that this kind of behavior is not acceptable. It would be easy for Lucille to continue trying to protect him, this time from the punishment of the law. But she and Ben must stand together and allow the law to give Clay a wake-up call.

Assuming that Ben and Lucille can come to a place where they can agree on Clay's discipline, their personal arguments should be minimized. Once Ben realizes that Clay's anger is not about him, he can work with it without becoming angry or defensive himself. Ben indicates that he still loves Lucille; together they need to face the future.

Look at your situation. Glean tools and techniques from Ben and Lucille's story to apply at your house.

Commitment

Noted management guru Peter Drucker says, "Unless commitment is made, there are only promises and hopes . . . but no plans." I find that this applies perfectly here. Unless Ben is committed to the marriage, to Lucille and to Clay and Nancy, they have only promises and hope. As an important step in the plan, Ben needs to hang in there.

While that is easier said than done, all those who have responded encourage Ben—and all stepfather's in this place—that it does get better. Clay may be testing him: Will the love Ben exhibited and invested during the courtship of his mother last? Will Ben resort to abusive behavior like Clay's father?

As additional encouragement, Chuck likes to point out to stepfathers that if they are the ones bringing up the child, they are the real parents, regardless of blood. The Bible shows a long genealogy for Christ—forty-two generations—leading up to Joseph (Matt. 1:1–17). However, Joseph was not the biological father of Jesus; he was, in effect, his stepfather. Yet, Joseph raised him as his own. Nowhere in Scripture does it indicate that Joseph was any less important in the life of Jesus than Mary—whose blood Christ did share. Joseph loved Jesus extravagantly. He didn't do it because Jesus was his bloodline, but because God called him to do it.

The study notes of the *Women's Study Bible* say,

> We can learn from Joseph three important qualities for godly stepparents:
>
> He did what the Lord asked him to do (Matthew 1:24);
>
> He allowed others to give good things to the child in his care (Matthew 2:11);
>
> He acted quickly to protect his child (Matthew 2:14–15).[1]

By marrying Lucille, Ben accepted God's call to be Clay's "real" father. Chuck has learned by working with children that to a child, the "real" father is the one who fulfills the role: "He took me to a baseball game, like a real dad." Young children do not distinguish between the father whose seed birthed them and the one who brings them up. However, our adult minds view the "real" dad as the sperm donor. This is something that adults have taught children as a means of positioning. In working with blended families, the concept of real parent versus stepparent is false and needs to be broken.

It is human nature to favor your own bloodline. Loving extravagantly allows God's nature to dominate by becoming the real father to the children He has placed in your care. With this in mind, when Clay acts out, telling Ben, "You are not my real father!" Ben needs to respond with extravagant love by saying, "You are my real son." This addresses the true emotional need of Clay rather than being caught up in a power struggle.

In Bev's childhood family, this adjustment was not an easy process. Reflecting on the relationship of her brother and stepfather, she says,

> It was a struggle, but when my brother graduated from high school several years later, he thanked my stepfather for making it possible. He knew he probably would have been in jail if he had continued the way he'd been going. My stepfather had already raised two lovely daughters. It was extremely difficult to try to raise a son who was already half grown. Many times I know he felt like giving up, but he held on. The struggle was worth what was achieved.

Overconnection

As a part of hanging in there and getting Clay on the right path, Michelle Holman, MA, LPC, encourages Lucille to look at her relationship with Clay.

> She may need to confess any improper emotional relationship she has had with him. A counselor may be needed to help them establish a healthy relationship and to walk with Clay to help him grieve the loss of the overconnection. In cases like this, the parent has often become a "god" in the eyes of the child. One parent is all good, while the other is all bad.

Jan found this was true with her daughters. As a Popular Sanguine, she sought to soothe their hurt by creating "fun" togetherness, especially shopping at the mall.

> Trying to be both mother and father, I way overbonded with my girls. Through counseling, I learned it was unhealthy for us. Besides, my budget couldn't take much more. I had to learn to cut the umbilical cord.

Stay the Course

Chuck advises stepfathers in Ben's circumstances to stay the course and ride it out. Leaving will not solve the problems and is apt to make them worse. As we have seen, Richard hung in with his son and got him through high school. Bev's stepfather stood firm and held her brother accountable, getting him through high school and finally receiving the thanks for his efforts.

With commitment, Ben can plan to help Clay live out his promise and hope. There is no guarantee that Clay will get through high school, that he will ever thank Ben, or that he will ever truly appreciate all his stepfather has done for him, but Ben needs to make that effort and he needs to make his marriage commitment a priority.

In *Sacred Marriage,* Gary Thomas reminds us that it may not be easy, that work is bound to be required to make our marriage work.

> When we get married, we make a certain promise to our spouse that we will devote a considerable amount of energy, initiative and time into building and nurturing the relationship.... When marriage is placed within the context of God's redemptive plan, we stay married.[2]

When Jan and Carl married, both of Jan's daughters were adults, yet they still had trouble accepting him as stepfather.

> We've had many battles in the last five years. Carl has remained consistent in his love for me and supportive yet firm in our joint family decisions. The girls have come to respect his com-

mon sense and now introduce him as their dad. He has been the stabilizing factor we needed.

Gene and Lynn made a commitment to each other when they entered into marriage, the second marriage for both. Gene had three children—ages thirteen, fifteen, and nineteen—who lived with their mother in a different state. Lynn had two children, ages thirteen and sixteen. Both lived with her. Gene reports his situation—somewhat like Ben's,

> After we were married, everything was fine—for the first few months. Then teenage rebellion hit. Lynn's son had been "man of the house" since her divorce eight years earlier. Since we married, I had not disciplined either of her children.

One night Gene came home to Lynn's son giving her a tongue-lashing about something he refused to do.

> I did not interfere in that heated exchange, but the argument continued and the situation escalated. I decided to take action.

Gene reports that he walked in on them and stood nose-to-nose with his stepson. He demanded,

> You will not talk to your mother like that anymore. Do you understand?

With fire in his eyes, Lynn's son informed Gene in no uncertain terms that he was not going to tell him what to do.

> When he shouted, "You are not my dad!" I calmly replied "Let me say it again. You will not talk to your mother like that anymore. Do you understand?" Then, I turned and walked to the bedroom and closed the door. After a few minutes, there was a knock at the door. He asked if he could come in. I opened the

door and was greeted with a hug. With tears streaming down his face, he cried, "I love you. I'm sorry."

Gene and Lynn made a pact based on Mark 10:9: "What God has joined together, let not man separate" (NKJV). "That included the children," Gene says:

Years pass. Teenagers become adults. Relationships heal and grow. Between us we have five children who have blessed us with wonderful grandchildren who will also pass through those teenage years.

For Ben and Lucille, for you and your spouse, we encourage you to stand on that Scripture as well—to love each other extravagantly, not to get, but to give, even if you feel like giving up!

The Interactions

For couples in a similar situation to Ben and Lucille, Chuck would assign the following "homework" assignment:

1. Whenever possible, communicate that the direction of one parent reflects the support of the other:

   - Mother: "Your Father and I have decided ———"
   - Father: "Your Mother and I have decided ———"

   Whenever pressed by the teen, a good fallback position is "Let me check with your mother/father before I give you my decision."
2. Create a log of the child's attempts to split up or divide the parents. This will bring awareness to the family dynamic. For example, Clay might say to Lucille, "Ben tells me stupid stuff to do! Do I really have to sweep the driveway?" Always back the other parent up, even if you think they are wrong! Disagreement and discussion should take place between adults, away from the children. Never let the child rush you into making a decision.

3. The stepfather needs to facilitate the creation of a "dad" name for the stepchild to call him. For example, "Clay, it is important to me that you call me something like 'Dad.' I know you think of your birth father as 'Dad.' Is there something else you would be willing to call me, like 'Papa' or 'Pop?'" This gives the child permission to call the stepfather a dad. The stepfather has taken the emotional risk of rejection by taking the initiative here. The selected name should communicate respect while showing endearment. It should not be the parent's first name, nor should it be "Father" or "Sir," as they are too formal.
4. When the child says, "You can't tell me what to do, you're not my real father," respond with, "You're my real son. I can and will tell you what to do." The stepfather needs to refer to his stepson as "son." Place a hand on his shoulder or hug when appropriate. Healthy touch is very important for teen boys *and* girls.

Sixteen

Finding Your Place

Insecurity, Stepchildren Relationships

The Issue

Lila and Dennis have been married for about six years. It is a second marriage for each and they both have children from their previous marriages. Lila's sons live with them, and Dennis' daughters are with them every other weekend. Most of the time, she and Dennis have a good relationship and she feels secure in his love. However, the minute his girls walk in the door, they become number one, and Lila takes a backseat. She has stood by him through battles with his ex-wife and business struggles, yet when his daughters are present, she questions his love for her.

Dennis complains that Lila would like his daughters to simply disappear, which he says "will never happen" as they will always be a part of his life and they do come first. Lila feels hurt by Dennis' response. She feels tense and stressed for days before the girls arrive. As a result their marriage suffers. Lila snaps unnecessarily at Dennis, and the anger she feels has built up over the six years of their marriage. Lila feels that the more Dennis cares for the girls, the more her resentment builds. Her anger spills out onto his children, pushing them closer and closer to Dennis.

The Insights

Shuttling children back and forth between parents is usually accompanied by complications. Adding a stepparent brings an additional element into the mix that is seldom easy and often results in a variety of problems.

Glen T. Stanton, author of *Why Marriage Matters*, states that

> The roles of stepparent and stepchild are hard to define and the emotional attachment of these two parties is quite different from the emotional attachment between a biological or adoptive parent and child.[1]

It is no wonder that Lila is having some difficulties in her relationships with both her husband and her stepdaughters. Each relationship will need work to bring Lila, Dennis, and the girls into a stable and satisfying place. First we will look at the need a woman in Lila's place has for security and then at building a mutually respectful relationship between the stepmom and stepdaughters.

Insecurity

Whether or not Lila's feeling of insecurity is warranted, it is a valid feeling and one shared by many women in her place. Gaylen Larson, PhD, sees that as a natural and expected response.

> The way women are wired, they have a deep inner need for security. The number one need in females is for security—both financial and relational; this is seen in what is known as the nesting instinct. Just the fact that she has entered into a new marriage shakes up her equilibrium as she adjusts to her new husband. Adding his children into the picture exacerbates the situation. Men, on the other hand, are wired with a primary need to feel significant and important. On his own Dennis is not likely to see how Lila perceives the situation or understand her need for security.

This need is something that both partners in a situation similar to Lila and Dennis's will need to work at.

Rose Sweet is a pastoral counselor and the author of *How to Be First in a Second Marriage*. She says,

> Some people would be quick to point the finger at someone like Lila, citing her insecurity and jealous nature. Misguided advice such as "grow up," "get over it," "you're the adult," and "you're so insecure" only serve to make the Lilas of the world feel even more rejected and at the bottom of the totem pole.

While there may be some element of truth in the "grow up" statements, they are not the only solution. As Gaylen Larson explained, insecurity is to be expected in this situation. However, once Lila realizes the cycle she is on, which she has done in sharing her story, as the adult she needs to take some steps to correct the situation.

Sherrie, one of our peer advisors, confirms this in her story:

> After years of handling it all wrong, I cried out to God. He gave me some amazingly comforting words—grow up! I had to ask myself who the adults were in our situation.

Adjust Your Expectations

No matter how valid Lila's feelings are, she cannot expect the girls to "disappear." What she can do, however, is to adjust her expectations.

Understanding this was very helpful to Sherrie in adjusting her attitude. She reports,

> While change did not come overnight, I realized that Bob's children had visiting rights and a schedule long before I came along. It's as though they were playing catch in the proverbial park of life, having found their way together and sharing a survivors' bond. I strolled in out of the blue and said, "Hey, throw me the ball too!" Then I was saying, "No fair. I didn't get a

turn." Soon I tried stealing the ball, hiding it, and pouting on the sidelines. Finally, I demanded, "Include me, or else."

While women like Lila should not beat themselves up over their feelings of insecurity, neither should they wallow in them. Adjust your expectations and move on. Understanding and accepting your husband's longstanding relationship with his children will help you overcome insecurities.

Sherrie tried to put herself in her husband's place to help her adjust her attitude about her husband's children and their relationship.

> I asked myself, "If I were him, what would I want?" As I focused on Bob and thought about how I could serve him, the resentment gave way to love. I realized we would be together long after the kids were all grown and raising kids of their own. Could I not give them this time together?

Ah, the power of extravagant love—not to get, but to give!

In his book *Sacred Marriage*, Gary Thomas encourages slowing down long enough to look at someone else's needs.

> It just may be that God gives us the marriage relationship to moderate and redirect our dreams. Forced to compromise, we learn to reevaluate what's truly important. We are asked to reconsider our priorities and slow down long enough to look at someone else's opinion or needs.[2]

Remembering her own struggles, Pam encourages Lila,

> Sometimes we as second wives forget there are other people in our husband's life. Pray that God will give you insight into how to handle your feelings and the situation. I believe that if you change your attitude, it could change your husband's. We are having the whole crew—my husband's boys, my mom, and my daughter and her husband—over for Thanksgiving. This will

be the first time in nine years that both of our children will be with us for a holiday. They are all spending a couple of days with us. God answers prayers and heals the hearts of those who have been hurt so deeply.

Consider Her Needs

As Lila begins to make some changes of her own, hopefully Dennis will change as well—the existing equilibrium will change. First Dennis needs to remember that scripturally he and Lila are one. Genesis 2:24 says,

> This explains why a man leaves his father and mother and is joined to his wife, and the two are united into one (NLT).

With this in mind, Jean Cox-Turner, a registered nurse, parent educator, and stepparent advises our case couple, and anyone in the same situation,

> Dennis should include Lila in at least some of the activities with his daughters. He should sit down with the girls and tell them how much he loves them and how much he loves Lila. Lila is his wife and he wants them all to be a family.

Anyone in a similar situation can learn from Susan Rogers' advice to Dennis:

> You can help by reassuring Lila of your love and commitment to make this new family work. Remember to lift her up in front of the kids, to show appropriate affection for her, and to model the respect for her that you want your girls to have. Lila can be your best ally in this effort if she is reassured of your devotion with quality love.

Teach Respect

Chuck notes that the dynamic at play here is the fact that showing respect for Lila is the best thing Dennis can do to give his daughters a strong self-esteem. It is a win-win. Dennis has stated that his daughters are the most important. The best thing he can do for them is to give them a model that they will internalize: a good husband puts his wife first. The daughters win. Lila wins.

By observing this behavior, Dennis' girls will recreate it in their own marriages; they will select husbands who put them first. If one of them dates someone who does not show her respect, she will likely quit going out with the guy because Dennis' behavior will have taught them what to expect.

I think every parent wants their daughter to select a mate who values and respects her. By respecting Lila, Dennis has the opportunity to positively influence his daughters' future happiness.

Additionally, demanding that the daughters respect both their mother and stepmother will ultimately be good for their self-esteem. A non-custodial father may think that by putting his girls above their stepmother, he is helping them feel good about themselves, feel important and special to him. However, the best way for him to do this is to build up women in general and to invest in their lives by going to their games and recitals, for example, not by putting them above their stepmother and not by entering her into a power struggle.

Susan Rogers makes the following suggestions for men in Dennis' situation to help them model respect for their wives:

> Small blessings, like noticing what is needed and taking care of it without being asked or reminded by her, will go a long way in helping her to feel treasured. When she stresses, just listen. Ask God, "What is she feeling or thinking?" and then share with her what you have heard. A little empathy will push the "Ah-ha, he loves me" button. Anxiety goes down, and everyone can relax. The worst thing you can do is to get defensive, so avoid it— though this is where most men fall. Truly, her anxious words do not pose a threat to you, unless you allow them to do so.

Constructive Counseling

If you are in a similar place to that of our case history couple, Rose Sweet, one of our professional advisors suggests that you plan to have a few conversations together—alone and uninterrupted.

> Share, talk, and explore, but do not just dump emotions on each other. Be clear about identifying your fears, needs, and possible solutions. The wife should make a list of specific emotional, physical, and financial needs and give examples of how she'd like those met. When sharing needs with her husband, she should be open and ask him to come up with his own style, choice, or options in meeting those needs so he does not feel too controlled.

After several clear discussions about how to change the dynamics, if Dennis and Lila cannot come to agreement, it's probably time to re-educate themselves on the basics: what God expects from husbands/wives regarding their spouses' needs. He says a man is to love his wife in the same way Jesus loves the church—to love so extravagantly that he would lay down his life for her (Eph. 5:25). He does not say the same to the man in his role as a father. While it is assumed that most fathers love their children, they are not instructed by God to love their children in the same way they are asked to love their spouse. Instead, they are first commanded to teach, guide, and train the children (Deut. 6:7). As simple and as exaggerated as it sounds, a man should train his children in love, but be willing to die for his wife (if that's what it takes!)—the true definition of loving extravagantly.

God's order for the family is that Dennis and Lila are now one flesh. That relationship comes before the children. By putting Lila ahead of his daughters when they are in her home, Dennis is modeling godly order and is letting the girls know that they cannot rule over their stepmother.

Stepchildren Relationships

Dennis' daughters will always be a part of his life, as they should be. Beyond simply accepting that fact, the difficulty for Lila comes in figuring out what her role in their lives should be. Her resentful attitude is pushing them away.

Lila may be feeling the same things Sherrie felt in adjusting to her stepchildren and their presence in her life.

> I saw the resentment in their eyes and despised myself for being unable (or unwilling) to manage the awful feelings that percolated within me.

Rather than pushing the girls away, Lila needs to develop a relationship with them. Susan Rogers says,

> Yes, they will resist you, but in time they will appreciate the grace you extended to them during this difficult time. Blended families are by nature birthed in loss. The children enter the new family setting with fragile emotions and insecurities. They are not equipped to handle the losses and changes of the adult world. Yet they are expected to adapt, to hide their fears, and to pretend that this unnatural situation is A-okay. They are torn between their love for their father with a strong desire to please him and loyalty to their mother with a strong desire to keep the peace.

Georgia Shaffer encourages Lila to establish a relationship with her two stepdaughters.

> Start by finding one activity the three of you enjoy. It may be shopping, cooking, making candles, or going to the hair stylist. By focusing on that special activity, the conversation will begin to flow and the relationships gradually will be established.

Along those same lines, Sherrie shares what happened when she was willing to put herself in the children's shoes.

> I realized that no matter how much attention Bob gave them during the weekend visits, it could never make up for what was taken from them. They were innocently caught in the middle.

From her own experience, Kathy agrees:

> Whatever the circumstances were for their parent's divorce, children feel that they have lost the non-custodial parent. They may have some fears, real or imagined, just as Lila does.

To help the girls deal with their own fears and insecurities, Susan Rogers suggests:

> Try to create an environment for the girls where they feel at home and not like visitors. Let them have their own furniture, hair products, clothing, and other personal items in their own room, as well as a love note to await them each weekend. Hauling stuff back and forth just increases the feeling that this is not really their home, rather only a place to visit. All females need to feel they have a "spot," and they will be restless and insecure until they know deep within their hearts that this is their home, too. So make every effort and give it some time.

To help the girls deal with the loss and role confusion, Lila needs to develop an appropriate relationship with them. But what should that relationship be? Susan Rogers says,

> Put your efforts into being a good friend rather than focusing so much on being a good parent. Children of divorce need your special friendship, Lila, not your competition.

Adjusting to the new role is often difficult as stepchildren have another mother; she cannot take their mother's place or take claim to anything she has done in the past. Then what can the stepmother do? Sherrie found this approach worked very well for her:

> This may sound strange, but to keep myself from taking on an all-or-nothing attitude, I began to think of myself as the kids' aunt or Sunday school teacher. They didn't need or want another mother, but it wasn't unreasonable to expect that we could have a mutually respectful relationship. I leave all the instruction, correction, and guidance to Bob—I take on a supportive role. Before each visit I ask Bob what he has in mind for the weekend so I know what to expect.
>
> I began to view the weekends as the "guy's time." This was a choice that helped me lose those ugly feelings of jealousy and competition. It also gave me permission to work on my own projects or visit a friend—plans to look forward to. To keep continuity, we always have meals together and share at least one activity as a family unit.

Within Sherrie's comments are many valuable tips that she learned the hard way. Sherrie's concept of viewing herself as a Sunday school teacher or aunt is a great way to deal with the relationship, providing care while allowing room for growth. Many stepmothers try too hard to make the new family into their perception of the perfect "Brady Bunch" household.

While writing this chapter, I went to lunch with some friends. When I brought up the topic, one friend affirmed that she had tried too hard in the beginning. She tried to force the blended family, made up of adolescents, to take outings and vacations together, with dismal results. Upon hearing this, one of the other women at the table exclaimed, "Kids at that age don't want to be with their parents anyway, stepparent or otherwise!" So true, and in hindsight it seemed so obvious. But in an effort to do everything right, my friend tried too hard to make it all work. Sensing her frustration, her husband told her to relax, to not try so hard. She heeded his advice and has found things have gone much more smoothly.

Sherrie now says,

> I look forward to the visits. Interestingly, the boys are now eager to share themselves with me and seek my participation. My tank is filled by the joy I see in my husband's face as he freely enjoys his few days a month with his children. I am encouraged as well because I know the boys will be healthier adults as a result of the changes we've made.
>
> It seems like the topsy-turvy days of visitation awkwardness will never end, but they can smooth out and become enjoyable for everyone.

Wouldn't you like to look forward to the times when your stepchildren come to visit? Apply the combined wisdom as presented in this chapter and do the "homework" assignment so you can get off of the emotional roller coaster and have a secure and happy home for both husband and wife and stepchildren!

The Interactions

For couples in a similar situation to Dennis and Lila, Chuck would assign the following "homework" assignment:

For the Mother

1. Create a list with complete descriptions of what behaviors your husband should display in front of the girls that will make you feel like you are number one. For example: Open the car door for you; seat you at the table.
2. Build up the self-esteem of the girls by engaging them in age-appropriate activities that they enjoy. For example: take teens shopping for clothes or makeup if that is their focus; attend their athletic events if they are involved in sports.

For the Father

1. Use your treatment of your wife as a means of modeling how a husband treats his wife.
2. Create a list with complete descriptions of what behaviors you will display in front of the girls that will make you feel like your wife feels that she is number one. For example:
   - (Wrong) Father: "Lila, would you do the dishes so the girls and I can go to the movies?"
   - (Right) Father: "Okay, girls, I want you to clear the table and wash the dishes. When you're done, Lila will take you to the mall."

Epilogue

From the Head to the Heart

As you read through this book, I trust you are encouraged to know that you are not alone. Many couples face circumstances similar to the ones you are going through. It is my desire that reading about others who have faced difficulties, and lived through them, will offer you hope. Those who contributed their personal stories were eager to help someone else traveling down the same road. While your situation may look like you are in a dark tunnel, those who have been there before are reaching back, giving you their hand to guide you to the light on the other side.

Reading a book like this can make you aware that there is a problem and that the problem has a solution. It can give you hope. But to apply what you learn, to see a difference in your situation, takes more than hope. It takes a desire and willingness to change.

This book is full of plans and projects. You can read them, then close the book and put it on a shelf. While I appreciate you buying the book, and I am grateful that you read it, I wrote it to help you. I assume that you bought this book because you have a need.

As you have read the previous pages, you may have seen symptoms similar to ones reflected in your marriage. Like the marriages described here, you, too, have a modern marriage. You, too, have some complications from which you'd like relief. Reading the scenarios and their proposed prescriptions may have brought up issues that you had not yet thought about. But what is important is what you do from here. It is all about change.

The Theory of Change

People read books and close the cover. They may even mean to apply the ideas that sparked their interest. A change may occur for a few weeks and then most people slip back into their previous patterns.

People go for counseling. They affirm the adjustments. In front of the counselor they agree to the approach. They walk out the door and go right back to their old ways.

Does this make self-help books wrong? Does this mean that counseling is ineffective? No. But it does mean that for you to see real changes in your marriage relationship, for you to make the reading of this book more than a simple exercise, it must go from your head to your heart. You must have a real desire for a changed heart.

Creating a Change in Your Life

Whether talking about our health, our faith, or our marriage, instituting change is hard work. We need to go beyond the head, beyond first order change—not just seeking change for symptom relief, but from the desire of a changed heart. Hard work can bring about second order change and a reordering of a person's life.

To bring about this level of change usually requires constant re-immersion. Going to the health club once will not change your physique. Even sporadic visits will produce no visible changes. However, a regular routine—reordering your life—is effective. Similarly, reading a book will not give you an improved marriage.

Because this deeper level of change does require a reordering of your life, each of the chapters has been presented in a clear problem/solution format. We desire that as you read the scenarios and consider your own situation, you project your own marriage into the setting. Then, as you read over the suggested solutions, the "insights," you see how to apply these answers to your own situation.

Write a New Chapter

Chuck strongly suggests that you reread the applicable chapters with your spouse. If your problem is different from any presented, use a chapter as a model to formulate your own chapter. Together write out what a therapist like Chuck would call a problem statement. This is a judgment-free description of the problem that reflects the perspectives of both parties. The problem statement does not place blame on either party and describes the situation as an unbiased observer would see it—objectively and free of criticism. This model helps you view the problem from a solution-focused perspective, moving you from blame to solution. Chances are it will reflect the scenarios addressed in this book, but as every marriage is unique, your problem statement will be different from another couple with a similar situation.

Next, write out what the problem will look like when it gets better. We call this a "compass statement" as it guides you to the end point. For example, using a few of the scenarios from the previous pages, a problem statement might be, "Louise resents their money going to the ex-spouse" or "The marriage lacks connectedness; instead it feels more like a business." After discussion, the description of what it will look like when the problem is better, the compass statement, might be, "The ex-wife is no longer a divisive issue; the issue changes to a challenge they face together." Or, "We will know the marriage is better when 'the two are one flesh' as evidenced by: both parties agree the value of the marital bond exceeds the value of material assets."

Once you have developed your problem statement and your compass statement, a good counselor or other wise advisor can help you brainstorm different hypotheses on why the problem exists. This hypothesis would point toward how to tackle the problem. Using the same scenario, the hypothesis might be: "Out of guilt and a desire to pacify his ex-wife, Darren agreed to a divorce settlement without the benefit of legal counsel. In order to avoid conflict or guilt, Darren continues to write 'one more check' each month. The long-term consequence of this financial drain is building resentment in Louise."

Once you have created the problem statement, the compass statement, and the hypothesis or hypotheses that will help clarify the situation, then select a solution or "insight" for action that tests—confirming or disproving—the validity of the hypothesis. Often the insights themselves bring about change with movement toward the compass statement. In other cases, different solutions to the problem must be thought out, tried, and evaluated. If you are trying to develop these statements on your own, be sure to seek the wise counsel of friends, family, or others who know you—such as your pastor.

Reorder Your Life

Throughout the previous pages, we have presented different possible solutions for a variety of situations. Bringing together a team of experts to review each scenario, we have brainstormed and developed several premises throughout each chapter. As the two of you review the appropriate scenarios and relate them to your own life, select the solution that most closely reflects your needs and will bring about the desired change. Review this process, re-immersing yourself in it frequently to see how you are progressing. Change can be measured by how far you have moved toward the compass statement, your definition of *better*.

Because reordering your life, bringing about second order change, does take work (just like getting in better physical health or developing a stronger spiritual life), there are exercises ("The Interactions") at the end of each chapter. These activities will help keep you focused on your process of change. Do not skip over them if you hope to see a true change of heart. Go back and, using a journal or blank paper, work through the exercises. Write your own project; be creative!

Being willing to make these deeper changes is what this book is all about. You change your heart attitude from getting to giving.

A Good Start

Some people will be strong enough and disciplined enough to make this heart level change on their own, just like the few regulars who show up at the gym, do their routine, and see results. But most will need some form of assistance and accountability. A book like this may be all the assistance some people need. In their quest for improved health, some have a strong enough desire for change that they only need one visit with the trainer to show them what to do. From there, they carry on. Others will need good nourishment to aid their progress, and still others will need regular visits with a trainer or coach to help them stay on track. I liken this process to the health club environment because it is easy to see the different levels of progress and help. If a person truly desires to make changes in their physical well-being, they need more than lifting weights, more than working out. They need good nourishment.

For us with the goal of improved marital health, this book is like your initial visit with your personal trainer, giving you hope and getting you on the right track. The good nourishment is the power of the Holy Spirit. Human nature is to be blinded to our own issues. We can read about them, see steps that would be helpful, but skip right over them choosing to believe that they do not apply to us. We do this with Scripture. We can read passages many times and not have them impact our lives. But through the power of the Holy Spirit, we may read the verse and it appears to us in a whole new light. It seems to jump off the page and hit us in the face. This is what happened for me when I read through Ephesians and came to "love extravagantly." Romans 8:5 affirms this:

> For those who live according to the flesh have their outlook shaped by the things of the flesh, but those who live according to the Spirit have their outlook shaped by the things of the Spirit. (NET)

Begin with Prayer

Before you and your spouse go back through the previous pages and read the scenarios that are applicable to you, be prayerful together. Ask God to help you remove any denial that may be present in your part of the problem. Ask Him to cause the situations that apply to you to "hit you in the face." John 14:26 promises us that He can do this for us. "The Holy Spirit, whom the Father will send in My name, He will teach you all things, and bring to your remembrance all things . . ." (NKJV). Oswald Chambers describes it this way,

> We think we understand another person's struggle until God reveals the same shortcomings in our lives. There are vast areas of stubbornness and ignorance the Holy Spirit has to reveal in each of us.[1]

With the power of the Holy Spirit nourishing you, allow this book to be your personal trainer, showing you on what areas you need to work.

Get a Personal Trainer

If you still find yourself repeatedly going back to old habits, you may need regular visits with a "personal trainer" to keep you accountable and offer guidance.

This is where an unbiased third party can be very valuable. This can be a friend (if he or she can be unbiased), a marriage accountability group, a pastoral counselor, or a professional therapist. Chuck has found that many times a couple will leave a session happy with each other, but angry with him. Confronting others with their issues is a dirty job, but when a third party is involved, anger can be directed at the counselor and stay there rather than going home with the couple. Some people can bring about change on their own, others need counseling. This does not make one a better or lesser person, rather this is merely an indication of our differences.

Marriage accountability groups can also supply valuable support to any marriage, from a couple ready to divorce to a couple who just wants a deeper, intimate relationship.

Being in a small group, or desiring a healthy marriage, or committing to accountability in our lives is nothing new—but doing those three things together is. That's why the new paradigm of marriage accountability groups is built on a different set of values.[2]

Consider an Accountability Group

Stephanie has contributed to many of the scenarios in this book. As lay leaders, she and her husband Kurt call their group "MAGNETS." MAG stands for marriage accountability group. The NET represents a "net" to catch them if they fall. Talking about their group, Stephanie says,

> The old paradigm embodied isolation, facades, fairness... judging and/or silence, but the new paradigm suggests community, genuineness, integrity, growth, and speaking the truth in love. Just like going to the gym or losing weight, we seem to stick to the program better sometimes if we do it with friends.

If you find that you need the guidance and accountability that a third party can offer, Chuck has several suggestions for selecting a therapist and making the time with your "personal trainer" successful (app. D).

From Head Change to Heart Change

Chuck worked with high-risk youth in a residential treatment facility. The boys he specifically worked with were all violent offenders who were one step away from jail. In the program, they received their education, their meals, lodging, and therapy. For most of these teenagers, their only motivation to change was fear of consequences, resulting in first order change at best. For the most part, the courts mandated their presence at the treatment center. The counseling appeared to do some good, but at the first opportunity, they reverted back to their old ways—like the Sunday Christian, their change was on the surface. However, a few of the young men had become Christians somewhere along the line. With the power of the Holy Spirit combined with the therapeutic efforts, real changes were made—changes that went from the head to the heart that played out in behavior.

For you, reading a book is a good first step—you understand the need for change, it is in your head. As a Christian, take advantage of the power that is available to nourish you and help you make real changes, reorder your life, and turn from your old ways—a changed heart.

Appendix A

Your Personality Profile

Popular Sanguines

"Let's Do It the Fun Way"

Desire: have fun
Emotional needs: attention, affection, approval, acceptance
Key strengths: ability to talk about anything at any time at any place, bubbling personality, optimism, sense of humor, storytelling ability, enjoyment of people
Key weaknesses: disorganized, can't remember details or names, exaggerates, not serious about anything, trusts others to do the work, too gullible and naive
Get depressed when: life is no fun and no one seems to love them
Are afraid of: being unpopular or bored, having to live by the clock, having to keep a record of money spent
Like people who: listen and laugh, praise and approve
Dislike people who: criticize, don't respond to their humor, don't think they are cute
Are valuable in work for: colorful creativity, optimism, light touch, cheering up others, entertaining

Could improve if they: got organized, didn't talk so much, learned to tell time

As leaders they: excite, persuade, and inspire others; exude charm and entertain; are forgetful and poor on follow-through

Tend to marry: Perfect Melancholies who are sensitive and serious, but whom they quickly tire of having to cheer up and by whom they soon tire of being made to feel inadequate or stupid

Reaction to stress: leave the scene, go shopping, find a fun group, create excuses, blame others

Recognized by their: constant talking, loud volume, bright eyes

Powerful Cholerics

"Let's Do It My Way"

Desire: have control

Emotional needs: sense of obedience, appreciation for accomplishments, credit for ability

Key strengths: ability to take charge of anything instantly and to make quick, correct judgments

Key weaknesses: too bossy, domineering, autocratic, insensitive, impatient, unwilling to delegate or give credit to others

Get depressed when: life is out of control and people won't do things their way

Are afraid of: losing control of anything (e.g., losing a job, not being promoted, becoming seriously ill, having a rebellious child or unsupportive mate)

Like people who: are supportive and submissive, see things their way, cooperate quickly, let them take credit

Dislike people who: are lazy and not interested in working constantly, buck their authority, become independent, aren't loyal

Are valuable in work because they: can accomplish more than anyone else in a shorter time, are usually right

Could improve if they: allowed others to make decisions, delegated authority, became more patient, didn't expect everyone to produce as they do

As leaders they have: a natural feel for being in charge, a quick sense of what will work, a sincere belief in their ability to achieve, a potential to overwhelm less aggressive people

Tend to marry: Peaceful Phlegmatics who will quietly obey and not buck their authority, but who never accomplish enough or get excited over their projects

Reaction to stress: tighten control, work harder, exercise more, get rid of the offender

Recognized by their: fast-moving approach, quick grab for control, self-confidence, restless and overpowering attitude

Perfect Melancholies

"Let's Do It the Right Way"

Desire: have it right

Emotional needs: sense of stability, space, silence, sensitivity, support

Key strengths: ability to organize and set long-range goals, have high standards and ideals, analyze deeply

Key weaknesses: easily depressed, too much time on preparation, too focused on details, remembers negatives, suspicious of others

Get depressed when: life is out of order, standards aren't met, and no one seems to care

Are afraid of: no one understanding how they really feel, making a mistake, having to compromise standards

Like people who: are serious, intellectual, deep, and will carry on a sensible conversation

Dislike people who: are lightweights, forgetful, late, disorganized, superficial, prevaricating, and unpredictable

Are valuable in work for: sense of detail, love of analysis, follow-through, high standards of performance, compassion for the hurting

Could improve if they: didn't take life quite so seriously, didn't insist others be perfectionists

As leaders they: organize well, are sensitive to people's feelings, have deep creativity, want quality performance

Tend to marry: Popular Sanguines for their outgoing personality and social skills, but whom they soon attempt to quiet and get on a schedule

Reaction to stress: withdraw, get lost in a book, become depressed, give up, recount the problems

Recognized by their: serious and sensitive nature, well-mannered approach, self-deprecating comments, meticulous and well-groomed looks

Peaceful Phlegmatic

"Let's Do It the Easy Way"

Desire: avoid conflict, keep peace

Emotional needs: sense of respect, feeling of worth, understanding, emotional support

Key strengths: balance, even disposition, dry sense of humor, pleasing personality

Key weaknesses: lack of decisiveness, enthusiasm, and energy; a hidden will of iron

Get depressed when: life is full of conflict, they have to face a personal confrontation, no one wants to help, the buck stops with them

Are afraid of: having to deal with a major personal problem, being left holding the bag, making major changes

Like people who: will make decisions for them, will recognize their strengths, will not ignore them, will give them respect

Dislike people who: are too pushy, too loud, and expect too much of them.

Are valuable in work because they: mediate between contentious people, objectively solve problems

Could improve if they: set goals and became self-motivated, were willing to do more and move faster than expected, could face their own problems as well as they handle those of others

As leaders they: keep calm, cool, and collected; don't make impulsive decisions; are well-liked and inoffensive; won't cause trouble; don't often come up with brilliant new ideas

Tend to marry: Powerful Cholerics who are strong and decisive, but by whom they soon tire of being pushed around and looked down upon

Reaction to stress: hide from it, watch TV, eat, tune out life

Recognized by their: calm approach, relaxed posture (sitting or leaning when possible)

For additional information on the personalities, read *Personality Puzzle* by Florence Littauer and Marita Littauer (Grand Rapids: Revell, 1992); *Your Spiritual Personality: Using the Strengths of Your Personality to Deepen Your Relationship with God* by Marita Littauer with Betty Southard (San Francisco: Jossey-Bass, 2005); and *Wired That Way* by Marita Littauer (Nashville: Regal, forthcoming). They are all available through your favorite booksellers.

Appendix B

Directory of Professional Contributors

Shellie Arnold
Author, *Return to Eden Resources: Reclaiming God's Vision for Family Relationships*
2200 Lake Lena Blvd.
Auburndale, FL 33823
shelliearn@aol.com

Sylvia Burke, BSN
Author, *Putting Humpty Dumpty Back Together Again*
25821 Bolero Ben
Rio Verde, AZ 85263

Evelyn Davison
Radio host, "LoveTalk"; publisher, *Good News Journal*; author, *Praying for America's Leaders*
9701 Copper Creek
Austin, TX 78729
(512) 260-1800
goodnews@aol.com

Roseanne R. Elling, MEd, LPC
Family and Individual Therapist
17103 Preston Rd., Ste. #288
Dallas, TX 75248
(972) 250-0498
(972) 250-0934 Fax
roseanne2000@aol.com

Reese Gateley, CPA
Tax and financial statement preparer and consultant for individuals and businesses.
4316 Carlisle Blvd. NE, Ste. C
Albuquerque, NM 87107
(505) 883-9221
(505) 884-3104 Fax
rgateley@gateleycpa.com

Michelle A. Holman-Nietert, MA, LPC
Christian Life Coach
Her Life, Inc.
3013 Conner Ln.
Wylie, TX 75098
(812) 319-3434
(972) 234-3059 Fax
www.michelleholman.net
mholman@swbell.net

G. Victoria Jackson, MSW, LCSW
Over thirty years of family counseling experience; teacher of cultural diversity and social work, Loma Linda University; contributing author, *Understanding Intimate Violence*; and co-founder, Touch of Class—a Christian charm course for teens in San Bernardino, CA
vjackson@univ.llu.edu

Directory of Professional Contributors 237

Stephanie and Kurt Janke
Walk in the Spirit
4949 East Gray St.
Mesa, AZ 85205
J7saphire@msn.com

Ruth L. Kopp, MD
Author, *Encounter With Terminal Illness* (with Stephen Sorenson), reissued as *When Someone You Love Is Dying* (Zondervan, 1980), and *Where Has Grandpa Gone* (Zondervan, 1983); family practice physician, emphasis on counseling
328 South 4th Street
Pekin, IL 61554
(888) 275-9766
(309) 347-1109 Fax
www.drruthmd.com
drruth@drruthmd.com

Gaylen B. Larson, PhD
Founder, California's largest professional counseling service; author; speaker; and consultant
26381 Crown Valley Parkway, Ste. 200
Mission Viejo, CA 92691-6301
(949) 474-4888
www.AskDoctorGaylen.com

Maxine Marsolini
Pastor's wife and author, *Blended Families: Creating Harmony as You Build a New Home Life* (Moody Press, 2000)
(503) 698-1211
mmarsoline@aol.com

Susan M. Rogers, MA, LPC
Director of CHPM Counseling Center
1420 Twin Oakes
Wichita Falls, TX 76302
(940) 696-0181
smrogers@chpminc.org

Georgia Shaffer, MA
Author, *A Gift of Mourning Glories: Restoring Your Life After Loss* (Servant Publications, 2000); Pennsylvania licensed psychologist; member of American Association of Christian Counselors; and executive director of Mourning Glory Ministries
P.O. Box 3113
York, PA 17402-0113
(717) 266-4773
(717) 266-7481 Fax
www.GeorgiaShaffer.com
Georgia@MourningGlory.org

Rose Sweet
Author, *How to Be First in a Second Marriage* (College Press, 1998) and *Healing the Heartbreak of Divorce* (Hendrickson Publishers, 2001); pastoral counselor; and member of American Association of Christian Counselors
73-241 Hwy 111, #3D
Palm Desert, CA 92260
(760) 346-9401
(760) 340-9430 Fax
rosesweet523@aol.com
www.rosesweet.org

Mary Hunt Webb, MA
Adult Learning and Training Specialist
P. O. Box 14462
Albuquerque, NM 87191-4462
mamswebb@highfiber.com

Directory of Professional Contributors

Melanie R. Wilson, PhD
Licensed psychologist, New Life Clinics of St. Louis, and director of marital preparation, Christ Memorial Lutheran Church
5252 South Lindbergh
St. Louis, MO 63126
(314) 707-6510
www.drmelaniewilson.com
melphd@aol.com

Appendix C

The Couple's Communication Exercise

*C*onsider *how you learned to communicate. Think of your family of origin, the parents talked at the children. In school, the teacher talked at the students. Perhaps you participated in classroom debate where persuasive speech was an asset. Throughout college and on into the work force, the skill of persuasive speech was rewarded. However, the skills that are functional in other aspects of our lives can be counter-productive within the marriage environment.*

Therefore, in preparation for growth within the marriage relationship, the weakest part of our communication skills (listening) must be developed. Where before we were either speaking or thinking about what we were going to say next, instead we will learn to focus on the other person. This basic skill for improved communication is called "active listening." In this process, we are not thinking about our response to what was said. We are not thinking about whether what our spouse is saying is right or wrong or even if we agree or disagree. We are only striving to hear and understand the words that are being spoken.

From a personality standpoint, some people inherently talk too much and others too little. The following exercise is designed to make communication a two-way street between opposite personalities. As in tennis, the ball should go back and forth, spending equal amounts of time on each side of the court with each party alternating turns. We are not advocating that this be the daily communication; rather, this is a specific exercise designed to strengthen a designated skill.

The Communication Exercise

This active listening exercise begins with person "A" making an "I" statement: "I feel," "I think," "I am," etc. The primary objective is to avoid the word "you." Husband and wife alternate playing "A" and "B." Chuck recommends that this "I" statement be constructed in a brief and concise three-point outline. Both parties need to turn toward each other and maintain eye contact throughout delivery of the statement. For example, using the scenario from chapter 5, Joan would face John, look him in the eye, and say, "I feel alone, neglected, and I really need more time together."

The goal for person B (this play John, next play Joan will be "B") is to strive to function as a tape recorder, reflecting back only what was said in an impartial manner. Person B should preface his response with "What I heard you say was . . ." Therefore, the complete response would be, "What I heard you say was, you are feeling alone, neglected, and you need more time together." Then, person B should always close his reflection with "How did I do?" This sets the stage for a subjective response from person A. It says, "I care more about what you feel than being right (or wrong) myself." Marriage is not a court of law; couples must get away from establishing truth or fact, and move on to pleasing each other.

Person A, Joan, should make a judgment call at this point. Either she is happy with the reflection or it fell short of her expectation. If she was happy with it, she says, "Very good," and the first play of the exercise is done. However, in reality more common response from person B would be, "You think I am neglecting you and I work too much"—which is not at all what she said. As in this case, if the reflection is inaccurate or involves a judgment, she should say, "That is not quite what I had hoped to communicate. May I tell you again?" This last, "May I tell you again?" is said with enthusiasm. This process continues until person B gets it right. Chuck has found that couples sometimes will go through a dozen cycles before a simple statement such as we have illustrated here is accurately reflected. This in itself is a victory.

Next, the husband becomes person A. He presents his feelings on a fresh tack without responding to her statement or defending himself. For example, he might say, "I feel trapped. At work they always want more. At home I feel guilty." She now responds, as person B, by reflecting exactly what he said, "What I heard you say is, you feel trapped. At work they always want more. At home you feel guilty."

This may seem contrived and elementary. However, many times Chuck has seen an exchange like the one above when a spouse says with excitement, "Yes! That's exactly what I've been trying to tell you for six years!" In other cases, person A will say in reflection, "Did I say that? I don't think that!" Most people have no idea how they sound to other people. Most people will not even recognize their own voices recorded on a tape recorder!

Once each partner has successfully stated their feelings and reflected them back to the other party several times, the exercise is complete. No resolution takes place at this stage. The goal is simply to exercise the listening skill, which will pay off in many other settings. In fact, whenever a party recognizes that their communication has become dysfunctional, this is a good fallback position to get back on track. It is virtually impossible to fight in this format.

The goal is for the marital relationship to become a mirror of the self. A mirror reflects a face in an impartial manner. Only within the intimacy of a healthy marriage (or therapy) can we begin to throw out our innermost thoughts and feelings, and examine them out in the open.

In most communication settings outside of marriage, the listener does not have our best interest in mind. What others say to us is focused on how they can persuade or control us. The marriage should be a safe haven from the world where we must surround ourselves with shields. However, within the marriage we must learn to lower these shields.

Appendix D

Choosing and Working with a Therapist

In receiving counseling you are in essence buying an intangible product. While the product (your marriage and/or your mental health) is of great value, its intangible quality makes it difficult to think of paying for it. You are dealing with your life; do not take the cheapest route.

First, screen your therapist. Ask the therapist about his or her education. Did she receive her training from a reputable institution with time-tested successes or was she involved in a home-study type program? Does the program have the accreditation or approval of organizations such as the American Association for Marriage and Family Therapy (AAMFT)? Was there a practicum in the program where the student counseled people while under the "live supervision" of a professor? Next, ask about his internship. Where was this done? What type of licensed therapist provided supervision? Were there mentors? At what point did he select a theoretical orientation? How is the therapist licensed? What is the therapist doing in continuing education? Ask the therapist/candidate: "What is your theoretical model of how change occurs?" There are many good answers here; any number of tools properly implemented will do the job. However, most therapists will not even understand the question, or will not have a clear answer. Look for a therapist who is excited about the change-oriented process.

Next, inquire about the therapist's motivation. Chuck remembers his education:

> My professor of law and ethics said the cleanest motivation for a therapist to perform therapy was in exchange for payment. The therapist does his job well and in return the customer pays a fee. This was controversial in our class. Most of my classmates felt that the motivation for therapy should be more altruistic. I agree with my professor. Beware of the therapist who is driven to "help people." Many of those with the greatest personal pathology feel the greatest need to meddle in other people's lives. Their own unresolved issues unavoidably color their patient's therapy.

Next, look at your own motivation. Do you have a real desire for change? Most people seeking professional help say they want to change when what they really want is relief from the consequences of their actions, an alleviation of symptoms. Some people do not want to change at all; they merely want an affirmation of their actions, or they seek counseling to humor someone else. If the therapist is unable to "fix" the problem, the client can then report that they tried: "I went to counseling, but it didn't work." The person who desires a real heart change invites the Holy Spirit into the process: "He convinces of sin; He illuminates and instructs."[1]

To make the best of your investment in counseling, be sure that you have a well-trained Christian therapist who has a change-oriented approach. Ask for referrals to find a therapist who has healthy motivation. Last, be sure that you go into counseling with a right attitude—allowing the Holy Spirit to convince you of sin, illuminate it, and instruct. While psychotherapy can fail, it doesn't have to.

Endnotes

Introduction: Marriage: A New Script

1. If you are unfamiliar with my teaching on the personalities—Popular Sanguine, Powerful Choleric, Perfect Melancholy, and Peaceful Phlegmatic, please read appendix A before going on.

Chapter 1: The Fire's Gone Out

1. Willard Harley, *His Needs, Her Needs* (Old Tappan, N.J.: Revell, 1986), 41.
2. Stormie Omartian, *The Power of a Praying Wife* (Eugene, Ore.: Harvest House, 1997), 65.
3. Ibid., 61–62.

Chapter 3: Childless by Choice

1. Jan Coleman, "Married Without Children: A Curse or a Call?" forthcoming in *Light and Life* (n.d.).
2. Roger and Robin Sonnenberg, *Living with Infertility* (St. Louis, Mo.: Concordia Publishing House, 1994).

Chapter 4: Growing Apart

1. Gary Thomas, *Sacred Marriage* (Grand Rapids: Zondervan, 2000), 35.
2. Dan Allender and Tremper Longman, *Intimate Allies* (Wheaton, Ill.: Tyndale House, 1995).

Chapter 6: Rocky Roads

1. *Life Application Study Bible* (Wheaton, Ill.: Tyndale House, 1997).
2. Peter Mayle, *Encore Provence: New Adventures in the South of France* (New York: Alfred A. Knopf, 1999), 79–80. (Special thanks to Lynn Morrisey for finding this quote for me.)

Chapter 7: Sacrificed Her Career

1. Michelle McKinney Hammond, *The Power of Femininity* (Eugene, Ore.: Harvest House, 1999), 233.

Chapter 12: Secret Spending

1. Gary Thomas, *Sacred Marriage* (Grand Rapids: Zondervan, 2000), 115.

Chapter 14: Deep Resentment on a Delicate Subject

1. Dorothy Patterson, ed., *Women's Study Bible* (Nashville: Thomas Nelson, 1995), 1583.
2. Gary Thomas, *Sacred Marriage* (Grand Rapids: Zondervan, 2000), 161.

Chapter 15: Between a Rock and a Hard Place

1. Dorothy Patterson, ed., *Women's Study Bible* (Nashville: Thomas Nelson, 1995), 71.
2. Gary Thomas, *Sacred Marriage* (Grand Rapids: Zondervan, 2000), 250, 262.

Chapter 16: Finding Your Place

1. Glen T. Stanton, *Why Marriage Matters* (Colorado Springs: Piñon Press, 1997), 158.
2. Gary Thomas, *Sacred Marriage* (Grand Rapids: Zondervan, 2000), 261.

Epilogue: From the Head to the Heart

1. Oswald Chambers, *My Utmost for His Highest,* updated ed. in today's language (Grand Rapids: Discovery House, 1992), reading for January 13.
2. Jeff and Lora Helton, *Authentic Marriages: How to Connect with Other Couples Through a Marriage Accountability Group* (Chicago: Moody, 1999), 36.

Appendix D: Choosing and Working with a Therapist

1. Charles Spurgeon, *Morning and Evening* (Grand Rapids: Zondervan, 1989), evening reading for October 12.

The Praying Wives Club
Gather Your Girlfriends and Pray for Your Marriage
By Marita Littauer & Dianne Anderson

Whether newly married or seasoned veterans, wives all over the country are discovering Praying Wives Clubs as a way to blanket their marriages in prayer. Featuring Scripture prayers, prayer request forms, and personality overviews, this book is both the story of women touched by God, and a helpful guide to beginning your own Praying Wives Club.

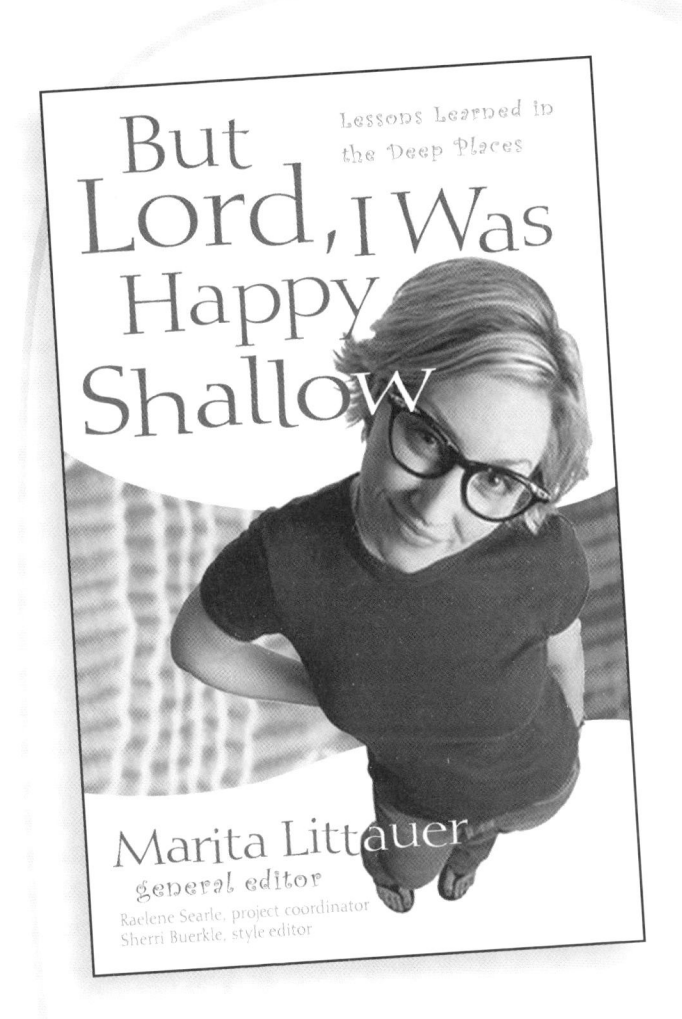

But Lord, I Was Happy Shallow
Lessons Learned in the Deep Places
Edited by Marita Littauer

This book, developed by the president of CLASServices, is more than a collection of meaningful stories; it is a light yet powerful affirmation of those lessons learned in difficult places. After all, some of the most laughable things now are those we cried about.